Advanced Praise

"So, if the philosophy of scientific materialism is wrong, can we conclude that God does exist? Does it mean that God is scientifically verifiable? That there is, in fact, a physics of God? Selbie makes a concise and convincing case that there is. He draws from the transcendent testimony of mystics the world over as well as from the findings of string theory, David Bohm's version of quantum physics, quantum biology, neuroscience, and quantum physics itself to demonstrate that a physics of God is at hand!"

—Amit Goswami, author of *The Self Aware Universe* and presenter in the award-winning movie, *What the Bleep Do We Know?*

"Selbie takes complex scientific subjects, and not only make them easy to understand, but shows us how we can apply them to live a better, fuller, richer life today. He unifies the teachings of the saints, provides a clear context for NDEs, and reveals the spiritual foundation that is hidden in today's sciences. Selbie paints a beautiful, uplifting and compelling picture of that which is felt by all but strangely unknown to many. This age of great science, made mute by material skepticism, is finally given a voice and a form in The Physics of God. It couldn't be more timely or timeless."

—Walter Cruttenden, author of *Lost Star of Myth and Time*

"This treasure of a book can radically change the way you see life. *The Physics of God* masterfully unites science and religion, while revealing the underlying principles of the universe and of our existence."

—Joseph Bharat Cornell, author of *Sharing Nature* and *The Sky and Earth Touched Me*

"It is essentially an article of faith among scientists that consciousness somehow arises in the brain and as such must be a product of evolution. This stubborn insistence that physical brain processes must be the source of consciousness will sooner or later prove to be a deadend. What will take its place, Selbie predicts, is recognition that consciousness is the only thing that is real, is the source of the apparent physical world, and is by its nature spiritual. Once we understand that all is consciousness manifesting in different ways, a whole new worldview will open up for mankind."

—Bernard Haisch, astrophysicist, author of *The God Theory* and *The Purpose-Guided Universe*

Unifying Quantum Physics,
Consciousness, M-Theory, Heaven,
Neuroscience, and Transcendence

The Physics
of God

JOSEPH SELBIE

FOREWORD BY
AMIT GOSWAMI

This edition first published in 2018 by New Page Books, an imprint of
Red Wheel/Weiser, LLC
With offices at:
65 Parker Street, Suite 7
Newburyport, MA 01950
www.redwheelweiser.com
www.newpagebooks.com

ISBN: 978-1-63265-110-5

Library of Congress Cataloging-in-Publication Data

Names: Selbie, Joseph, author.
Title: The physics of God : unifying quantum physics, consciousness,
    M-theory, heaven, neuroscience, and transcendence / by Joseph Selbie ;
    foreword by Amit Goswami.
Description: Wayne : Career Press, 2017. | Includes bibliographical
    references and index.
Identifiers: LCCN 2017032453 (print) | LCCN 2017038290 (ebook) | ISBN
    9781632658968 (ebook) | ISBN 9781632651105 (pbk.)
Subjects: LCSH: Religion and science.
Classification: LCC BL240.3 (ebook) | LCC BL240.3 .S45 2017 (print) | DDC
    201/.65--dc23
LC record available at https://lccn.loc.gov/2017032453

Cover design by Howard Grossman/12E Design
Cover photograph © agsandrew/depositphotos
Interior by Gina Schenck

Printed in the United States of America
IBI
10 9 8 7 6 5 4 3 2 1

DEDICATION

This book is dedicated to all the scientists who have courageously explored outside the unofficial boundaries of scientific materialism, and to the saints, mystics, and near-death experiencers who have engagingly shared their transcendent experiences of realities beyond the material.

ACKNOWLEDGMENTS

I would like to thank my many friends and well-wishers who encouraged me by saying, "I can't wait to read it!" It helped keep me going through the occasional fourth rewrite of an entire chapter. Special thanks to Amit Goswami for generously helping me "join the club." Heart-felt thanks go to two editors: Prakash van Cleave, who, through his edits, is always patiently teaching me the art of clarity, and Sharron Dorr, former editor for Quest Books, whose astute questions made the book even clearer. To M.C., Y.S., A.S., and C.S.—you didn't know it but you helped a lot—I had mental conversations with all of you to see if you would find my arguments convincing. (As far as I could tell, you did.) And last, I want to give my loving thanks to my wife, Lakshmi, my first reader and insightful critic. I always looked forward to her saying, "Well, I read the chapter. . . ." I knew the ensuing conversation would be lively.

CONTENTS

CONTENTS

FOREWORD

Joseph Selbie's *The Physics of God* is a unique and welcome addition to the growing literature for the scientific evidence for God. Why is this important? To begin with, it runs counter to a misconceived bias that has dominated scientific thought now for several centuries.

In the 17th century, Isaac Newton gave us a mathematical science that all but eliminated the idea of God intervening in the material world of physics and chemistry. In the same century another scientist, René Descarte, laid the foundation for championing the use of reason to develop the natural sciences. Ever since then (and following the prevalent notion of Christianity, actually), Western scientists have generally held the notion that animals are machines. This intellectual attitude stands true even today—that is, almost.

In the 19th century, Charles Darwin's theory of biological evolution suggested that living beings have a hereditary component (which we now recognize as genes) that undergoes changes called "mutation." Through the process of natural selection, nature selects among these variations those that help the species to adapt to the ever-changing environment; in time, this process leads to speciation. Since Western science maintained that animals are machines, and Darwin was saying that we are descendants of monkeys, doesn't it follow that humans are machines, too?

When later genes were experimentally discovered and even the structure of the DNA molecule of which genes are part was figured out, the view grew that biology is nothing but an extension of chemistry. Biologists and most other scientists with them assumed that everything about life will sooner or later be unraveled by the science of biology—leaving nothing for God to do! God's intervention even in the affairs of the living seemed to have been ruled out.

In the 20th century, a few scientists (Einstein, for example) held on to the idea of a benign God in what is called the philosophy of "Deism." But the notion that God is dead took hold in the scientific mainstream that soon promulgated the idea of a new philosophy by which to do science—scientific materialism. This philosophy says that every phenomenon is a material phenomenon in space and time caused by material interaction. There is nothing but matter!

This philosophy is clearly a dogma; Selbie calls it a religion, correctly I think. It has given humanity a polarized perspective, torn between God and materialist science, the world over and specifically with dire consequences in America. Selbie addresses this polarization directly and adroitly, showing how science and religion, far from being incompatible, share a deep congruence.

Scientific materialists thought seriously through much of the 20th century that life itself will be produced in the laboratory from nonliving matter, putting the whole question of whether God is needed or not to rest. Unfortunately, despite biology's many spectacular successes, the questions of "What is life?" and "Can life be produced from nonlife?" have remained unanswered. Meanwhile, Darwin's theory itself has come under fire with revelations that suggest that it really does not explain the details of available fossil data.

Other compelling data exists against scientific materialism. In scientific materialism, all communication is local, via signals. But as this author and many others have discussed, there is much evidence in favor of signal-less—that is, nonlocal—communication both in the micro and the macro domain of matter. Among such signal-less communications are distance viewing and near-death experiences. Especially the latter is spectacular: The evidence proves that there is consciousness even after the brain dies. So consciousness has to occur even before the brain exists, right? *Exactly*.

Some of the most compelling evidence against scientific materialism has come from quantum physics, the latest paradigm of physics that has replaced Newtonian physics. In quantum physics, objects are waves of possibility that reside in a domain of reality called "the domain of potentiality" where communication is instantaneous, without signal, nonlocal. This domain must be outside the realms of space and time where locality reigns. Nonlocal phenomena are referred to as "paranormal" by the mainstream scientists, but that designation is obviously prejudiced in light of quantum physics.

So, if the philosophy of scientific materialism is wrong, can we conclude that God does exist? Does it mean that God is scientifically verifiable? That there is, in fact, a physics of God? Selbie makes a concise and convincing case that there is. He draws from the transcendent testimony of mystics the world over as well as from the findings of string theory, David Bohm's version of quantum physics, quantum biology, neuroscience, and quantum physics itself to demonstrate that a physics of God is at hand!

In my own view as a quantum physicist, quantum physics alone gives us God, but my personal view is beside the point. The point is that any serious thinking person can look at the data and the existing ideas of post-materialist thinking and figure out that God is back in science. Drawing on the work of leading scientists as well as leading mystics, Selbie has provided a wonderfully persuasive and clear argument for coming to that conclusion.

The most important point is that with God back in the picture and backed up by science this time, we can go about founding a human science in which all human experiences are legitimate and scientific, including the spiritual. Others and I are working on that, and I am glad that Selbie has joined the effort! Read this book; it will help you, too, to gain this new perspective. The only qualification is that you see yourself as more than the soulless machines that many scientific materialists see. The rest, as Selbie describes it, is the beginning of life's greatest adventure.

—Amit Goswami, quantum physicist

INTRODUCTION

A love of science came to me early and has stayed with me all my life. My family tree is full of doctors and engineers. My father studied at Princeton, Harvard, and MIT. My brother graduated from Georgia Tech. Dinner-table conversation at home had to be backed up with references. In my college entrance exams I was in the 99th percentile in science and math. I entered the University of Colorado confidently expecting to land a science degree, and I spent most of my first two years studying math, physics, microbiology, and chemistry.

Then something happened that forever altered my course in life: I had a transcendent experience.

Like many of my generation, I experimented with psychedelic drugs. In one life-transforming "trip" I had an utterly beguiling experience. I became—to my delight—highly intuitive, serenely calm, and warmly heart-centered. My awareness subtly expanded to take in everything from the glow of life in a plant to the hidden feelings of my companions. I felt myself to be more than a body. At the heart of my experience were expansive feelings of boundless peace, joy, and well-being, feelings that seemed completely natural, as if the person I had always been simply woke up. I had never felt more joyful, more alive, or more at peace in all my life.

It was beyond wonderful.

The experience stayed with me for several days—long after any trace of the drug could have remained in my system. I realized then that the drug could only have *triggered* the experience and that the *source* of that experience had to be an integral part of who I am. The realization that my experience was not simply an ephemeral hallucination set me on a personal quest to find out how to live in that amazing transcendent state all the time.

There was nothing I knew about science—at that time—that could explain what I had experienced. Abruptly changing my major from microbiology to philosophy, I took a deep dive into Western metaphysics. Eagerly I immersed myself in Plato, Aristotle, Hume, Kierkegaard, Kant, Nietzsche, Sartre, and many Christian theologians, including Augustine and Aquinas. Though I found some inspiration in my several-year-long swim through Western philosophy, I did not find what I was hoping to find. Western philosophy tends to be drily intellectual. I learned almost nothing to help me bridge the gap between the heady thoughts of these philosophers and my heartfelt transcendent experience.

Not satisfied, I transferred to UC Berkeley, where I studied, with deepening interest, the philosophies of Buddhism, Jainism, Taoism, and Hinduism. These philosophies began to narrow the gap between theoretical knowledge and my actual transcendent experience because, unlike most of the Western philosophers, who relied on reason and logic to arrive at an *intellectual* understanding of consciousness and matter, the Eastern sages relied on methodical and repeated transcendent experiences to arrive at an *experiential* understanding of consciousness and matter.

The difference between the Western and Eastern approaches is like the difference between talking about a meal and eating one—and I soon learned that the secret to eating the meal is meditation. I was drawn to meditation for the same reasons I was drawn to science: It was precise, rational, and—most crucially—provided verifiable results. No belief required. Meditation is the objective instrument of discovery in what I've come to understand as the *science of religion*. In meditation, at last, I had discovered a practical and effective means of attaining the transcendent awareness and joy that I had only accidentally stumbled upon through my use of psychedelic drugs.

To my delight, I also discovered that embracing the science of religion did not mean that I had to abandon the science of matter. It did not mean that I had to cast aside the rational and the practical. It did not mean that I had to deny the findings of science. I found that the laws that govern the physical world are inextricably interconnected with the laws that govern the subtle world to which meditation gives one access. I realized that there is no conflict between science and religion at all: Those who use the science of religion to explore reality are simply using another method to discover the same truths as science reveals.

Let me share one intriguing example:

Annie Besant and Charles Leadbeater were prominent members of the Theosophical Society from 1895 to 1933. During that time they conducted, by means of deep meditation, investigations into the nature of atoms. They systematically observed many different types of atoms, ranging from gases to metals. They described and drew hundreds of diagrams of what they observed in a series of journals. (You can imagine how the notion of the psychic investigation of atoms was received by the particle-physics community in the 1920s!)

Several years after the passing of Besant and Leadbeater, physicist Steven M. Phillips studied their journals. He was struck by a recurring detail that appeared in many of their diagrams: They drew three dark areas in each proton and neutron in the nucleus of the atom. Today scientists believe that all protons and neutrons are made up of three quarks— but this was not known to science during the lifetimes of Besant and Leadbeater. Phillips concluded from this recurring depiction, and from other details in their journals, that Besant and Leadbeater had accurately described the number and nature of quarks years ahead of their discovery by modern physics. Dr. Phillips published his findings in the 1980 book, *Extra-Sensory Perception of Quarks*.[1]

Besant's and Leadbeater's ability to perceive the correct number of quarks in protons and neutrons highlights a fundamental premise of this book: There is—and can only be—*one* reality. Those versed in the science of religion, and those versed in the science of matter, simply use different methods to explore the same reality. Material scientists discover its properties through rigorously controlled experimentation and call it *reality*. Spiritual scientists discover its properties through rigorously controlled transcendent experience and call it *Reality*.

How to *unify* the findings of science and religion, however, is not immediately obvious, thus the need for books like this one. The two approaches—material science and religious science—use very different languages. On the surface, these languages—as different as words and math, parables and laws, allegories and theories—appear to describe two completely different realities. Compounding that difficulty are popular biases: Many people in science and many people in religion fervently deny that *their* reality could have *anything* to do with the other; like Victorian British aristocrats aghast at the thought of mixing with ignorant foreigners, they consider the divide between science and religion deep and absolute.

Yet, if we look deeper, if we set aside the pervasive material bias of science and lift the obscuring fog of religious sectarianism, we can find a surprisingly clear unity of science and religion. In this unity we discover that the explanations of transcendent phenomena given by enlightened saints and sages—miracles, life after death, heaven, God, and our ability to attain personal transcendent awareness—are matched by explanations of material phenomena given by scientists in the fields of relativity, quantum physics, medicine, string theory, neuroscience, and quantum biology.

In my decades-long exploration, I have come to appreciate that the findings of the science of religion and the findings of the science of matter—together—combine to give us the most complete view of reality: what I think of as the physics of God.

CHAPTER 1

The Religion of Science

Making a case for an underlying unity of science and religion would be pointless were it true that science had already ruled out any basis for the beliefs underlying religion. Unfortunately, many people, not just scientists, believe that it *is* true. There are strong voices among scientists who fervently proclaim that science has, indeed, *proven* that all religious beliefs are unfounded—that religion is simply keeping alive baseless superstitions and other nonsense.

At first glance their arguments are compelling. They invoke the scientific method. They tell us that none of religion's claims have been proven in the laboratory. They assure us that their arguments rest firmly on factual scientific discovery. They speak with utter conviction.

You will no doubt be surprised, therefore, and possibly affronted, when I say that the people who hold such absolute views are simply true believers in their own religion: *scientific materialism.*

Scientific materialism rests on the belief that everything there is or ever will be springs from the interactions of matter and energy—*and from absolutely nothing else.* Despite the existence of enduring major scientific mysteries, such as the origin of life and the nature of consciousness, scientific materialists believe that *it is only a matter of time* before all as-yet-unexplained phenomena will be explained by—and only by—the interactions of matter and energy.

This expectation is an article of *faith* among those who embrace scientific materialism. It is their *credo*. Given science's undeniable success over the last three centuries, scientific materialism's matter-and-energy-only hypothesis is very convincing to a lot of people. Science's means of exploring reality—the scientific method—is the oracle of the age. Using the scientific method, scientists have uncovered myriad laws governing the operation of the physical world. It is no exaggeration to say that the application of those laws over the last two centuries has *transformed* civilization.

Unfortunately for other religions, the religion of scientific materialism is in the ascendant and very influential. Not just many scientists, but also a huge percentage of people in the world, are unknowingly members of the church of scientific materialism because they have embraced the credo: Everything that is, or ever will be, is the result of matter-energy interactions and nothing else.

But make no mistake: The idea that everything that is and ever will be springs from the interactions of matter and energy—and nothing else—is a belief, not a proven fact. Despite the efficacy of the scientific method, it is not the case, as scientific materialists would have us think, that science has applied the scientific method to all possibilities for nonmaterial realities and proven them all false. Rather, science as an official body has become so convinced of the truth of scientific materialism that it simply doesn't explore alternative possibilities.

The bias toward material explanations for all phenomena is so strong that it nearly eliminates the possibility of funding for any scientific inquiry that attempts to explore realities other than the material. A vocal portion of scientists dismisses out of hand, or, worse yet, holds in disdain, even the *suggestion* that there may be nonmaterial solutions to unexplained phenomena. *Embracing* such a suggestion is not, to put it mildly, a path to a successful career in science.

I recently read an article by Sebastian Anthony in the online magazine *ExtremeTech*. (I picked it almost at random from many similar articles from which I could make the same point.) He cites a recent scientific paper published by Max Tegmark of MIT.[1] In his paper, Tegmark suggests that consciousness might be a quantum state of matter. What I found most interesting in the article was not the explanation of Tegmark's quantum state approach to consciousness but a comment by the article's author: "Consciousness has always been a tricky topic to broach scientifically. *In most serious scientific circles, merely mentioning consciousness might result in the rescinding of your credentials and immediate exile to the land of quacks and occultists* [italics added]."[2]

Another article, appearing this time in *Slate* magazine, also recently caught my eye: "Quantum and Consciousness Often Mean Nonsense," by Matthew Francis. The title itself speaks volumes. The author's patronizing tone in the article adds more volumes: "It sounds good at first: We don't know exactly how some things in quantum physics work, we don't know exactly how to go from the brain to consciousness, so maybe consciousness is quantum. The problem with this idea? It's almost certainly wrong."[3]

My favorite sentence, after Francis magnanimously, but ingenuously, admits that science may not know everything, is his emphatic declaration: "It's almost certainly wrong." Why? The answer to "why" isn't found in the current facts known to science but in Francis's belief that all phenomena will eventually be explained by scientific materialism. Such belief engenders the attitude that hypotheses of any other kind are simply a waste of time. If you read the article, you can feel his impatience with people who try to find nonmaterial solutions to still unexplained phenomena. "Don't they get it?" he seems to ask. "Don't they know all this nonmaterial stuff is ridiculous?"

Even rigorously conducted scientific studies that experiment with nonmaterial notions such as consciousness—those few that do somehow manage to get funded—are granted no credibility by science's high priesthood: the scientists who perform peer reviews, the approvers or rejecters of papers submitted to prestigious scientific journals such as the *Physical Review Letters*, *The New England Journal of Medicine*, or *Proceedings of the National Academy of Sciences.* You would be hard-pressed to find in these journals any papers that stray from the orthodox view of scientific materialism.

A case in point is the fate of several scientific papers that emerged from the Princeton Engineering Anomalies Research (PEAR) program. PEAR was founded in 1979 by Robert G. Jahn, then dean of the Princeton School of Engineering and Applied Science. Despite the pedigree of Princeton University and of Professor Jahn, and despite the overwhelmingly high quality of the science conducted, not one paper based on PEAR's successful proof of telekinesis was ever accepted by a respected scientific journal.[4]

PEAR's methodical practice of science was impeccable. PEAR conducted experiments for *27 years* to determine whether individuals could affect material objects without physical contact. Among their experimental approaches, PEAR developed a variety of what they called *random events generators* (REGs), such as water fountains, cascading steel balls, pendulums, and electronic systems. The REGs were rigorously developed to be impervious to all known outside influences such as vibration, pressure, temperature, and electromagnetism. No REGs were used in their experiments unless they had demonstrated precisely measurable results and maintained rock-solid consistency when left in isolation.

Once a REG was determined to have rock-solid consistency, volunteers were then asked to try to alter its rock-solid consistency by their thoughts alone. For example, volunteers tried, without touching or influencing the devices in any physical way, to make more water flow in one channel of a fountain than the other, or to make more steel balls cascade to one side of a device than the other.

PEAR conducted these experiments for almost three decades, using hundreds of volunteers, in thousands of experiments, accumulating billions of data points. The results of these experiments revealed that *nearly every volunteer had successfully altered the baseline distribution of the REG.* The change from the baseline was often miniscule—but consistent— *to an overwhelming statistically meaningful degree.* The odds against the possibility that PEAR's experimental findings are merely the result of random events are several *trillion* to one. In other words, practically speaking, there is no chance at all that their findings could be wrong: The volunteers successfully affected the behavior of physical systems using only their minds.

Yet no prestigious scientific journal ever published their papers. PEAR's findings, by every objective measure, were based on facts gathered in a stringently scientific manner. But because their findings fell outside scientific orthodoxy they were not given any scientific legitimacy.

There was recently a controversy when TED, the organization that presents talks by many leading-edge scientists and social thinkers, was pressured by a lobby of scientists to remove from its website talks given by Rupert Sheldrake and Graham Hancock. Sheldrake's talk presented 10 areas in which the scientific assumptions of today may be wrong. Hancock presented arguments for the independent existence of consciousness. At the insistence of a TED's advisory group of scientists, both talks were removed from TED's website by the organizers. After a storm of protest in favor of Sheldrake and Hancock, TED's organizers attempted to make peace with both sides by restoring the talks to a little-accessed archive of talks buried deep in TED's website.[5]

I watched both presentations. Both men made good arguments and offered facts to back up them up. In an ideal world, one in which the free discussion of ideas is allowed, these two talks would have been welcomed; instead they were banished to the margins of the Internet because they championed thoughts that fall outside the orthodox beliefs of scientific materialism.

Not content with merely passively defending scientific orthodoxy, there are a few scientists who believe that the best defense is an active offense. A number of scientists have personally mounted campaigns to position religious belief as ideas for the weak-minded, as socially destructive anachronistic behavior, or outright fraudulent manipulation of the gullible. Just a few examples of their book titles make my point: Richard

Dawkins's *The God Delusion*, Christopher Hitchen's *God Is Not Great: How Religion Poisons Everything*, and Victor Stenger's *God: The Failed Hypothesis; How Science Shows God Does Not Exist.*

These men are the self-appointed Grand Inquisitors of science. They try to debunk religion with a vengeance, lest members of their own flock should believe such heresy against science. Their claims have nothing to do with the scientific method and everything to do with the religion of science; their claims say far more about human nature than about science. These men have more in common with TV evangelism than with cool scientific objectivity.

Obscured by the notoriety of such men is the fact that most scientists are not scientific materialists. A 2009 Pew poll on religion found that only 41 percent of the scientists polled considered themselves to be atheists, while 51 percent believed in God, a universal spirit, or a higher power.[6] Also obscured by such strident and materialistically biased points of view is the fact that science's own findings—when viewed without material bias—are far from proving that religious beliefs are unfounded, and support the existence of transcendent realities such as consciousness.

In the early 20th century, physicists witnessed the emergence of numerous paradoxical discoveries that challenged, and still challenge, the core assumption of scientific materialism. Physicists discovered a hole in their understanding of matter—a gaping hole that came to be known as *quantum physics*—through which they fell to join Alice in Wonderland.

In the 1920s, physicists discovered that light can behave as either a particle or a wave. Later research revealed that not just light exhibits this dual behavior—matter can behave as a particle or a wave. And here is what especially makes the "gaping hole" gape: It became increasingly clear that light or matter only behave like particles *in the presence of an intelligent observer.*

If you are unfamiliar with quantum physics, what I just stated probably makes no sense to you at all, nor did it to the physicists of the 1920s. The discovery left physicists feeling they had joined the Mad Hatter's tea party. The best way I know how to explain the discovery is to walk you through an oft-repeated series of experiments. The counterintuitive results of these experiments never fail to leave people bemusedly shaking their heads—the experimental equivalent of talking to the Cheshire Cat.

These experiments are commonly known as double-slit experiments. Light's wave-like nature can be demonstrated by shining a single beam of light through two side-by-side vertical slits in a barrier (Figure 1), thus creating two new side-by-side beams of light. The two new beams of light will then fan out and interfere with each other like water waves in a pond. When water-wave troughs meet, they form a deeper trough. When water-wave crests meet, they form a higher crest. When troughs meet crests, they cancel each other out in proportion to their respective depths and heights.

Physicists, trying to understand the nature of light more fully, devised another double-slit experiment. Instead of shining a light continuously through the two slits, they developed a way to send one photon of light at a time through the slits. Since photons are the *particle* form of light, physicists expected to see a pattern form on the detector like the pattern bullets would make when fired from a gun into a target (Figure 2).

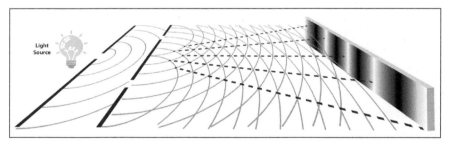

FIGURE 1. *Light shows its wavelike nature when it passes through the double slits and forms two new beams of light, which then interfere with each other in the same way as water waves. The image on the far right shows the characteristic interference pattern that forms on a detector. The brighter bands show where two wave crests meet and create a higher crest or two troughs meet and form a deeper trough. The darker bands show where crests meet troughs and partially or fully cancel each other out.*

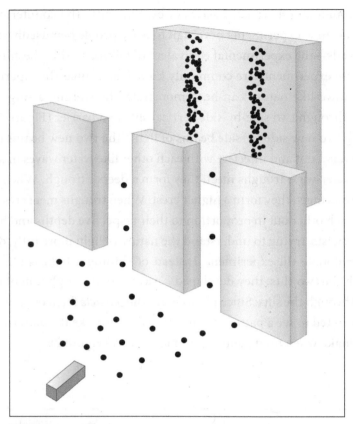

FIGURE 2. *What physicists expected to see on the detector—two bands of photon impacts comparable to bullets hitting a target.*

Imagine the experimenters' astonishment when, even though only one photon was released at a time, each photon still behaved as if it were part of a wave interfering with another wave (Figure 3). Such behavior doesn't seem possible, yet it has been confirmed in experiments again and again.

Begin playing *Twilight Zone* theme. . . .

Collectively scratching their heads, physicists tried to understand how this paradoxical result could occur. Eventually they conducted another experiment: a measuring device was placed by the slits to detect which slit an individual photon actually traveled through. (The measuring device does not interfere in any way with the passage of the photons through the slits.) Now try to imagine the experimenters' even deeper astonishment: Once the measuring device was added to the experiment, the photons passed through the slits and hit the detector like bullets fired from a gun (Figure 4).

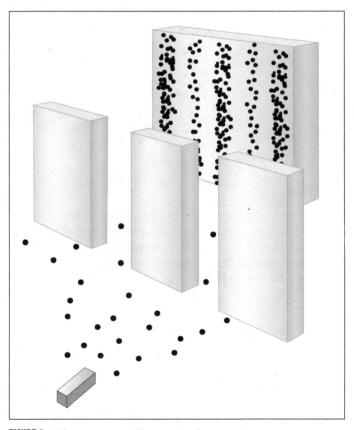

FIGURE 3. *What was actually seen in the experiments, even though the photons were sent one at a time through the slits, was the same interference pattern as one sees in Figure 1—a little rougher than the interference pattern created by a continuous light source, but unmistakably the same pattern.*

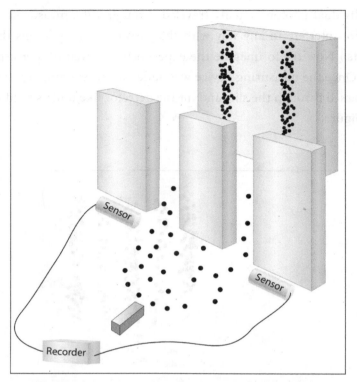

FIGURE 4. *Once the experiment was set up to measure which slit individual photons were passing through, the photons behaved like particles and created the pattern on the detector one would expect of little bits of matter.*

Why? Why did the photons behave differently? Nothing had changed! The *only* difference in the two experimental setups was that the passage of the photons through the slits had been *measured by an intelligent observer.*

Feel free to shake your head some more—and you can turn off the *Twilight Zone* music if it's bothering you.

Physicists have subsequently performed this same experiment, always with the same result, using atoms and molecules, objects trillions of times larger than photons. Physicists have gone on to prove, thousands of times, that until measured by an intelligent observer, everything—whether energy such as light, or matter such as atoms—behaves in a wavelike manner until measured by an intelligent observer. The inescapable conclusion: *An intelligent observer plays an essential role in the formation of matter.*

> There is no object in space-time without a conscious subject looking at it.
>
> —Amit Goswami, quantum physicist[7]

This discovery punched a huge hole in scientific materialism and sent shock waves through the scientific community. Niels Bohr (1885–1962), considered the father of quantum physics and a scientist whose reputation is only slightly less lofty than Einstein's (1879–1955), was among the first to conclude that physical objects do not have an independent, objective reality. He stated categorically that physical objects only appear when we observe them—and his assertion has never been disproven.

Welcome to Wonderland.

As a result of these discoveries, science went through an existential crisis. If matter has no fixed form until observed, if it exists in some insubstantial state until observed, then where does that leave science? As Albert Einstein said, likely speaking for most scientists, "I like to believe that the moon is there even if I am not looking at it." But according to the double-slit experiments, the moon *isn't* there unless one is looking at it. The old puzzler, "If a tree falls in the forest and no one is there does it make a sound?" had a new answer: If no one is there, there is no sound, there is no tree, there is no forest, there is no earth, there is *no thing*.

Science was saved from its existential crisis by the mathematics of probability. In the late 1920s and early 1930s, many brilliant physicists working across the world managed to build a mathematical bridge over the gaping hole created by the intelligent-observer paradox and other "quantum weirdness"—a bridge that allowed them, for all practical purposes, to get a free pass out of Wonderland and ignore the intelligent-observer conundrum.

They built the mathematical bridge by adding the mathematics of probability to a nascent mathematical system known as *quantum mechanics*, founded in 1900 by Max Planck (1858–1957). Despite its blending with the inexact-sounding world of probability theory, quantum mechanics is extremely accurate; it became, and remains, one of the most important scientific tools of the 20th and 21st centuries. It has been essential to the development of many marvels, including the advanced communications and computer science that enable so much of our civilization.

But don't misunderstand: Despite its undeniable success, the development of the equations of quantum mechanics only made it *unnecessary* to answer the deeper questions about the nature of reality raised by quantum physics; it didn't answer them. The vast majority of physicists—with a sigh of relief—moved on to the business of inventing things and quite happily left behind the mysteries surrounding the nature of reality raised by quantum physics. But deep mysteries regarding *the ultimate nature of reality* remain unsolved. As Berkeley physicist Nick Herbert wryly sums it up: "One of the best-kept secrets of science is that physicists have lost their grip on reality."[8]

In 1997, a poll was conducted among quantum physicists regarding what "quantum physics" actually means. The findings were written up in an article titled "A Snapshot of Foundational Attitudes toward Quantum Mechanics." The authors conclude: "Quantum [physics] is based on a clear mathematical apparatus, has enormous significance for the natural sciences, enjoys phenomenal predictive success. . . . Yet, nearly 90 years after the theory's development, there is still no consensus in the scientific community regarding the interpretation of the theory's foundational building blocks."[9]

The need for an intelligent observer is not the only hole in the argument for scientific materialism. When we look to the findings of the disciplines that deal most directly with life and consciousness, such as medicine and neurobiology, we find many more such holes.

In 1976, a randomized, controlled study of a potential chemotherapy treatment for gastric cancer was conducted by the British stomach cancer group. The results of the study were published in the May 1983 *World Journal of Surgery*.[10] Four hundred and eleven patients participated in a double-blind study that involved the use of placebos. Neither the patients—nor the clinicians—knew who received a placebo/saline drip treatment and who received the trial drug-drip treatment. During the course of the study, which lasted for several months, *30 percent of the patients who were given the placebo/saline drip treatment lost all their hair.*

More dramatic examples of mind affecting body can be found in studies of people suffering dissociative identity disorder (DID), more commonly known as multiple-personality disorder (MPD). Sufferers of multiple personalities have been closely studied. These individuals can change from one personality to another in minutes, even in seconds; they may change personalities as many as 10 times in a single hour. While multiple-personality disorder is well-known, what is less well-known is that the rapid personality changes are often accompanied by rapid physiological changes.

In his 1988 paper, *Psychophysiologic Aspects of Multiple Personality Disorder*, Dr. Philip M. Coons reviews more than 50 studies that identify physiological changes occurring when an individual with multiple personalities changes from one personality to another.[11] The studies have shown that one personality can be allergic to specific allergens, such as bee-sting toxin, and other personalities within the same individual are not allergic. One personality can be left-handed while other personalities are right-handed. One personality can have moles or scars that another does not. One personality can need glasses while others do not. In a 1985 study conducted by Shepard and Braun, the eyesight of one multiple-personality sufferer was thoroughly measured—refraction, visual acuity, ocular tension, keratometry, color vision, and visual fields—after each of 10 personality changes that took place in the course of one hour. Each personality's eyes were uniquely different—including, in one case, *the color of the iris.*[12]

One might argue that the placebo effect takes place over sufficiently long periods of time in order to explain our thoughts or feelings *triggering* known biochemical processes. In multiple-personality cases, however, no known biochemical processes can explain the *rapidity* of the physiological changes, much less changes that would normally be considered *genetically impossible*, such as a change in the color of the iris.

Yet another hole in scientific materialism's belief system is evidence that information can be exchanged from one mind to another. Oddly enough, some of the evidence comes from the CIA. During the 1970s and continuing until 1995, the CIA conducted a secret program called Stargate. The program's creation was motivated by Cold War fears. In the 1970s, the CIA believed that the Russians were training people to gather secret information remotely by means of psychic observations. If this "remote viewing" psychic ability *could* be developed, the CIA did not want to be at a disadvantage, and thus it started its own program. Eventually, the CIA had 22 different labs set up around the United States to test and develop this ability.

The CIA's Stargate program ran for more than 20 years. The program was abandoned in 1995 because the data gathered by its remote viewers was not *consistently* reliable enough to make it useful as an intelligence-gathering method—yet it *was* inconsistently valid. The American Institutes for Research's blue ribbon panel report concluded: "The foregoing observations provide a compelling argument against continuation of the program within the intelligence community. *Even though a statistically significant effect has been observed in the laboratory* [italics added]."[13]

Many people have interpreted the program's closure as proof that such psychic abilities do not exist *at all*, when, in fact, the program established that some remote viewers could properly identify images with a significant degree of accuracy. The problem for the CIA was that the degree of accuracy wasn't close enough to 100 percent to be trustworthy or useful. But the results were accurate to a degree that was far, far beyond chance, thus plausibly indicating that, in some scientifically unexplained way, the mind can directly receive information from outside the body.

Numerous such discoveries—the role of the intelligent observer in the formation of matter, instantaneous physiological changes among multiple-personality sufferers, PEAR's proof of telekinetic effects, the CIA's remote-viewing successes—collectively cast significant doubt on scientific materialism's belief that everything there is and ever will be is the result of matter-energy interactions, and have led many scientists to hold more thoughtful views as to the potential truth behind nonmaterial religious beliefs.

There are many highly regarded scientists who do not share the narrow view of scientific materialism's true believers. Nobel Prize winner Werner Heisenberg (1901–1976), a titan of early 20th-century physics, suggested that underlying all matter is an indivisible and unseen realm, for which he coined the term *Potentia*, and from which objects spring into existence when observed by an intelligent observer. Fellow of the Royal Society David Bohm (1917–1992), another well-regarded and highly influential physicist who was a scientist on the Manhattan Project and a pioneer in the study of quantum physics, came to believe that all reality is *inseparably interconnected*. In his book, *Wholeness and the Implicate Order*, Bohm convincingly—and mathematically—proves that no object can exist separately from any other.

John von Neumann (1903–1957), who is considered to be one of the greatest mathematicians of the 20th century and who was also a scientist on the Manhattan Project, asserts that consciousness doesn't merely affect reality; consciousness *creates* reality. And as counterintuitive as it may seem, von Neumann's views also rest on rigorous mathematics.

Pioneering British astrophysicist Sir Arthur Eddington (1882–1944) wrote in *The Nature of the Physical World*, "The stuff of the world is mind-stuff." He goes on:

It is necessary to keep reminding ourselves that all knowledge of our environment from which the world of physics is constructed, has entered in the form of messages transmitted along the nerves to the seat of consciousness. . . . It is difficult for the matter-of-fact physicist to accept the view that the substratum of everything is of mental character. But no one can deny that mind is the first and most direct thing in our experience, and all else is remote inference.[14]

Professors of physics Fritjof Capra, author of the *Tao of Physics*, and Amit Goswami, author of *The Self-Aware Universe*, represent some of the thinking of the newer generation of physicists who have been exposed to Eastern spiritual philosophies.

An increasing number of scientists are aware that mystical thought provides a consistent and relevant philosophical background to the theories of contemporary science, a conception of the world in which the scientific discoveries of men and women can be in perfect harmony with their spiritual aims and religious beliefs.
—Fritjof Capra[15]

Instead of positing that everything (including consciousness) is made of matter, this philosophy posits that everything (including matter) exists in and is manipulated from consciousness.
—Amit Goswami, quantum physicist[16]

You will hardly find one among the profounder sort of scientific minds without a peculiar religious feeling of his own. But it is different from the religion of the naive man. His religious feeling takes the form of a rapturous amazement at the harmony of natural law, which reveals an intelligence of such superiority that, compared with it, all the systematic thinking and acting of human beings is an utterly insignificant reflection.
—Albert Einstein[17]

These scientists are hardly "quacks and occultists." Among them are Nobel Prize winners and luminaries of physics whose numerous discoveries and mathematical formulations remain fundamental to modern science. For these scientists to even attempt to answer the deeper questions raised by their discoveries required them to grapple with concepts dealing with consciousness, thought, and perception—the traditional realm of philosophy and religion. Although their speculations are grounded in scientific logic and were arrived at methodically, rationally, and even mathematically, the concepts that emerge—interconnectedness, consciousness, higher intelligence—are decidedly nonmaterial.

Unlike true believers in scientific materialism such as Dawkins and Stenger, other more open-minded and expansive scientists go wherever the facts of science lead them. If the facts of science suggest there is more to reality than matter-energy interactions alone can explain, then so be it.

The material bias of science that leads many nonscientists, especially, to conclude that the beliefs underlying religion have been disproven, is just that: a bias extolled by a minority of scientists who believe in the religion of scientific materialism. But the fact is: Not one of religion's core beliefs—miracles, life after death, heaven, God, or the possibility of personal transcendent experience—has been ruled out by science. Rather, it is the widespread acceptance of scientific materialism's (unproven) *beliefs* that has made many people think so.

CHAPTER 2

The Science of Religion

Although it is true that science has by no means disproven the fundamental beliefs of religion, failure to disprove does not automatically make religion's beliefs true. How, then, can we decide whether or not there *is* any truth to religion's claims?

One way we can evaluate such claims is by comparing the testimony of those who have had profound transcendent experiences. When we look beyond the superficial variations of language, culture, and vocabulary such people use to describe their transcendent experiences, we find a compelling consistency.

Another way to evaluate the veracity of religion's claims is to study the remarkably similar ways in which the saints and sages attained such transcendent states. At the heart of all religions you will find men and women who practiced a universally effective *science of religion.*

The science of religion is a collection of disciplines, usable by anyone, which, when performed with determined focus and intention, inevitably result in personal transcendent experience. From personal transcendent experience come the revelations that give meaning to all religions. The disciplines that bring personal transcendent experience deserve to be considered scientific because they provide *consistent and repeatable results* when practiced to perfection.

I'll be the first to admit that it is difficult to see anything that looks remotely like science when one first examines the welter of precepts and tenets held by the orthodox believers of the myriad world religions. I have come to appreciate, however, that the bewildering and often contradictory mix of practices and beliefs surrounding religions reveals far more about human nature than it does about the transcendent nature of religion. It has been said that Christ was crucified once but his teachings have been crucified every day since. Through the centuries, Christ's words of unconditional love have been turned into rationales for prejudice, oppression, brutality, and war. The words of Buddha, Krishna, Mohammed, Lao Tzu, Moses, and countless other spiritual teachers have suffered similar fates.

The original and universal message of all true spiritual teachers is easily lost, or worse, twisted out of all recognition by the unfortunate tendency of people who want to have the corner on truth. This same unfortunate tendency is equally apparent in politics, sports fandom, and, as we've just explored, science—but in religion it is particularly intense and fervent. Orthodox religionists are much more concerned about proclaiming the differences of *their* religion (which, to them, are clearly superior) from all other religions than they are concerned in emphasizing shared truths. Worse yet, most orthodox religionists are unassailable in their belief that their religion, and their religion alone, is true.

Ironically, what is most obscured in the confusing fog of religious teachings and claims of exclusivism are the shared commonalities of the original teachings of the founders of the world's major religions, as well as of the thousands of Christian saints, Sufi masters, Zen roshis, Hindu savants, Taoist sages, Tibetan adepts, and independent mystics who have come after them. It is the testimony of these men and women that should interest us most, because it is *they* who have had the actual transcendent experiences from which all religion springs and by which it is perpetually refreshed.

Like Besant's and Leadbeater's uncanny ability to see at a subatomic level, these men and women demonstrated abilities and perceptions that go beyond the norm—intuitive knowledge, instantaneous healing, and material miracles. Further, and most tellingly, they all exhibited profound states of peace, harmony, and love to such a degree that, while they were alive, thousands of people were drawn to them like iron to a magnet. If we are clearly to see the science of religion amid orthodox religion's obscuring welter, it is to the experiences of these enlightened saints and sages that we should look.

> Theologians may quarrel, but the mystics of the world speak the same language, and the practices they follow lead to the same goal.
> —Eknath Easwaran, creator of Passage Meditation[1]

On close examination, one soon sees that all these enlightened saints and sages achieved their transcendent states by using variations on two indispensable practices: *stillness* and *inner absorption*. Stillness and inner absorption are the core disciplines of the science of religion. When practiced to perfection, they will *always* bring the practitioner—regardless of the practitioner's beliefs (or nonbelief), culture, gender, era, or stage of life—to transcendent, beyond-sensory awareness.

Stillness

The enlightened saints and sages of all religions disciplined themselves to be able to remain profoundly still for hours, days, and even weeks. Gautama Buddha is said to have sat beneath the Bodhi tree in determined meditation for 49 days. Jesus Christ spent 40 days in the desert in fasting and intense prayer. Accounts abound of Himalayan yogis, Zen masters, and Christian monks and nuns remaining locked in stillness for lengthy periods:

> Sit quietly, and listen for a voice that will say, "Be more silent." Die and be quiet.
> —Rumi, Sufi mystic[2]

Stillness is the altar of Spirit.

—Paramhansa Yogananda, yoga master and
author of *Autobiography of a Yogi*[3]

We need to be alone with God in silence to be renewed and transformed. In it we are filled with the energy of God himself that
makes us do all things with joy.

—Mother Teresa of Calcutta[4]

Be still and know that I am God.

—Psalms 46:10

Why the need for stillness? Spiritual teachers from all traditions say
the purpose of such profound stillness is to withdraw from bodily awareness, to withdraw from the continuous flood of information coming
through our senses, because it is the sensory flood that drowns out our
ability to perceive other, more subtle, but always present, realities.

Imagine you are attending a lively outdoor party in the country-
side. You are talking animatedly with others, dancing to loud music,
and eagerly eating and drinking, continuously immersed in strong sensory experiences. So dominant are these strong experiences that you are
unaware of milder input such as the sounds of birds, the warmth of the
sun, the scent of pine trees, or the subtle shades of color in the grasses
and plants. Although these more subtle inputs are just as present, you are
simply unaware of them because of the overwhelming effect of your more
pronounced sensory experiences.

My lively party analogy contrasts two different *intensities* of sensory
inputs: pronounced and subtle. Teachers of the science of religion contrast
two different *types* of input: sensory and transcendent. They tell us that in
profound stillness, as sensory input recedes from our awareness, we naturally become aware of transcendent realities that have always been present. There is a simple equation in the science of religion: The more still one
becomes, the more aware one becomes of transcendent realities.

Scientific studies confirm that deep states of stillness result in a pronounced shift in awareness away from sensory input and bodily awareness. In the late 1990s, leading neuroscientists Andrew Newberg, MD, and his (now deceased) colleague, Eugene D'Aquili, MD, studied the brains of Buddhist monks during meditation and of Christian nuns during intense prayer sessions.[5] They injected their subjects with a radioactive substance and then monitored their brain activity with single-photon emission computed tomography, or SPECT. They discovered that during their subjects' meditation or intense prayer sessions there was significantly decreased activity in *all* regions of the brain that process sensory information.

Of particular interest, they saw a significantly decreased level of activity in the *orientation association area* (OAA), located near the top of the brain. In our normal waking state, nerves constantly send information to the OAA, from which our brain provides us a continuously updated mental picture of our body's current position, orientation, sensations of temperature, points of contact with other objects, and so on. While in deep stillness, these nerves, normally stimulated by movement, stop sending new information to the OAA. This happens naturally when we fall asleep. When it occurs during the conscious practice of disciplined stillness, test subjects say that they became increasingly less aware of their bodies until many feel entirely bodiless.

Physical stillness also slows the metabolic processes of the body. Anyone who sits still for any reason will experience a decrease in heart and breath rate; stillness reduces the body's need to take in oxygen and to expel carbon dioxide. *Disciplined* stillness can slow the heart and breath rate below normally achievable levels. Many studies, such as, "Heart Rate Dynamics during Three Forms of Meditation," published in the *International Journal of Cardiology*, confirm the efficacy of such techniques to significantly slow breath and heart rate.[6] The practice of stillness can become so pronounced that the heart and breath can actually stop. Yogis in India have demonstrated the ability to remain breathless and without heartbeat for extreme periods. In 1973, a study was conducted at the Rabindranath Tagore Medical College and Hospital in Udapur, India.[7] An experienced yoga practitioner, Yogi Satyamurti, volunteered to be tested. While connected to a 12-lead electrocardiograph (ECG), he remained in continuous meditation for eight days. Soon after the experiment began, Yogi Satyamurti's heartbeat stopped altogether and did not resume until nearly the end of the eighth day.

Such experiences are not found only in the East. Saint Paul wrote, "I die daily" (I Cor. 15:31). Western spiritual teachers, such as St. Teresa of Avila, offer practices to intensify the experience and depth of prayer that will induce beyond normal stillness.[8]

A pleasant surprise for anyone, who by the practice of the science of religion achieves a deeper than normal state of stillness, even if only momentarily, is the accompanying result. Even beginners soon experience a relaxation of emotional tension, a sharpening of mental clarity, a feeling of well-being, and a strong sense of peace. And these results are just the beginning. Deep stillness allows the practitioner to experience feelings and states of awareness far beyond what most people can imagine.

Inner Absorption

Practitioners of the science of religion soon discover that one cannot achieve perfect physical stillness without achieving perfect mental and emotional stillness, and vice versa. The two are inextricably linked.

> Not till your thoughts cease all their branching here and there, not till you abandon all thoughts of seeking for something, not till your mind is motionless as wood or stone, will you be on the right road to the Gate.
>
> —Huang Po, Zen master[9]

> Still the bubbling mind; herein lies freedom and bliss eternal.
>
> —Swami Sivananda, yoga master[10]

To the mind that is still, the whole universe surrenders.

—Lao Tzu, *Tao Te Ching*

Anyone who has tried to meditate can attest to how readily the mind flits from thought to thought even when the body is relatively calm. Yogis wryly compare the experience to that of a drunken elephant randomly and unstoppably careening through the landscape of one's mind. Fortunately, enlightened saints and sages have passed on successful techniques and practices for subduing the drunken elephant. They fall into two broad categories, *devotion* and *concentration*: focusing the heart and focusing the mind.

Devotion can be described as the heartfelt determination to become absorbed in feeling. Mind and feeling are holistically linked. Thought tends to follow feeling—as anyone who has a strong desire can attest. The mind keeps returning to focus on strong feelings regardless of what else one might be trying to think about.

The primary tools of devotion are heartfelt prayer, devotional singing, and chanting. Such practices vary across religious traditions, but the common purpose is to awaken deep, determined yearning for God—in whatever form one holds dear. A Christian may focus on Jesus or Mary; a Hindu on Krishna or a goddess such as Lakshmi; a Buddhist on Buddha; a Muslim on the formless Allah.

Those who have a natural attunement to the heart find themselves able to forget themselves in their devotions. The small and random thoughts of the mind are eclipsed by powerful and sublime feelings. Caught up in devotion, all else is forgotten—including the body and all sensory input.

In addition to such devotional practices, the enlightened saints and sages, particularly of the East, offer techniques for concentrating the mind. These techniques often involve the mental repetition of phrases, or *mantras*. Some techniques involve watching the breath or breathing in deliberate patterns. Many require a steady focus of one's attention at the point between the eyebrows. Generally we can say that all of these are techniques of meditation. Those who employ such techniques regularly can become so mentally focused that, as in the practice of devotion, the practitioner loses awareness of the body.

Many scientific studies have been conducted to measure the effects of meditation and prayer. Subjects from all religions and mystical traditions, from Catholic nuns to Zen monks, have participated in such studies. The subjects' brain activities have been measured using, among other devices, EEGs (electroencephalography), fMRIs (functional magnetic resonance imaging), and SPECT (single-photon emission computed tomography). These measuring devices detect increases or decreases in brain activity in *specific* parts of the brain (fMRI and SPECT) or, in the case of the EEG, detect changes in *overall* brain activity.

Brain activity, as measured by an EEG, is typically categorized into alpha, beta, delta, and theta brainwave rhythms. Broadly speaking, our everyday, physically active state of consciousness tends to produce a beta-wave rhythm. Restful, deep thinking tends to produce an alpha-wave rhythm. Deep sleep produces a delta-wave rhythm. Meditation, too, produces an alpha-wave rhythm, which, as mentioned, is generated when people concentrate or think deeply. However, meditators often pass through the alpha-wave rhythm, like a stage in a process, to arrive at theta-wave rhythms.

Theta waves have been detected when people are dreaming deeply (REM sleep), learning, visualizing, or creating. Theta-wave rhythms, also detected in deep meditation, are thus associated with what we might call motionless, but highly focused, activity, revealing that meditation is far more than a pleasant wander through one's thoughts. Deep meditation is profoundly engaging, creative, and focused.

The electroencephalogram is only able, however, to measure the overall electrical activity in the brain. Other techniques, particularly functional magnetic resonance imaging (fMRI), allow scientists to measure activity taking place in specific areas of the brain and thereby provide us a deeper view of the effects of meditation.

Activated areas of the brain—areas with increased blood flow—appear to "light up" on the fMRI's computer screen. Studies using fMRI scanning have given us a thorough map of the specific areas of the brain that light up when subjects perform specific activities. We know, for example, which parts of the brain become *active* when the body is in motion or when the senses are actively engaged. We know which parts of the brain become active when solving problems or being creative. We know which parts of the brain light up when various emotions are stimulated from sexual arousal to loving kindness.

We also know which parts of the brain become active, and which become inactive, when people meditate, practice concentration, or practice devotion. During meditation, the areas of the brain that process sensory information and physical movement become *inactive*. These areas include those which receive sensory input from specific body parts and those involved in motor control, spatial sense, speech, and primal emotions such as fear and anxiety. These areas are located in the parietal, occipital, and temporal lobes, in the back of the brain, as well as the cerebellum and brainstem (Figure 5).

During meditation, the areas associated with attention, creativity, and the finer emotions, such as love and compassion, become active. These areas are located in the frontal lobe of the brain, including, especially, the prefrontal cortex that lights up when we concentrate (Figure 6). It is in this area of the brain that we orchestrate thoughts in accordance with our goals. The frontal lobe, especially the prefrontal cortex, is also associated with our higher abilities: imagination, creativity, appreciation of art and music, problem-solving, planning, conscience, manners, and morals. Activation of our highest qualities lights up the frontal lobe. The converse is also true: When we activate the frontal lobe through meditation, our highest qualities are activated as well.

It is also interesting, in light of the many devotional techniques that are used in the science of religion, that the frontal lobe includes the

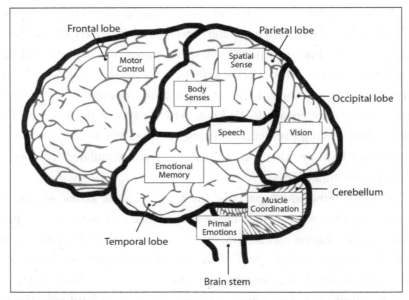

FIGURE 5. *The parietal, occipital, and temporal lobes in the back of the brain, as well as the cerebellum and brain stem become inactive during meditation. These areas of the brain are associated with sensory input from specific body parts and those involved in motor control, spatial sense, speech, and primal emotions such as fear and anxiety.*

specific areas of the limbic system—the system of our brain that processes emotions—that are activated by feelings of compassion and empathy.

Parts of the limbic system are activated during the formation and processing of *any* emotion. The limbic system activates during emotional responses of the most primal—fear, aggression, hatred—as well as when we experience finer feelings—peace, compassion, love. However, primal feelings activate the lower-most areas of the limbic system, known as the brain stem, while finer feelings activate higher areas of the limbic system, close to the frontal lobe, which include the cingulate cortex, hippocampus, and thalamus. The anterior cingulate cortex especially, that part of the cingulate cortex that is in closest contact to the frontal lobe, has been associated in numerous studies with empathy and compassion (Figure 6).[11]

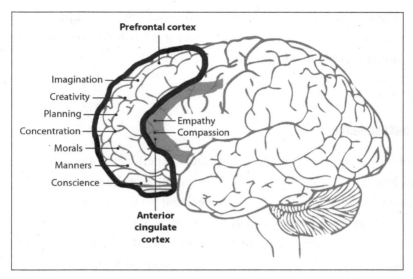

FIGURE 6. *The prefrontal cortex and the anterior cingulate cortex become activated during meditation. These areas of the brain are associated with attention, creativity, and the finer emotions, such as love and compassion.*

While science can quantitatively measure brain waves and detect what parts of the brain are activated during states of concentration and devotion, we must rely on the testimony of meditators and practitioners of devotion to describe the experience qualitatively. Universally, they describe their experiences as far more rich, far more expanded, far more *real*, than anything they experience in their normal waking lives.

> When we raise ourselves through meditation to what unites us with the spirit, we quicken something within us that is eternal and unlimited by birth and death. Once we have experienced this eternal part in us, we can no longer doubt its existence. Meditation is thus the way to knowing and beholding the eternal, indestructible, essential center of our being.
>
> —Rudolf Steiner, mystic and founder of Anthroposophy[12]

The kingdom of God does not arrive when we are looking for it, nor do they say, "Here it is," or "There it is." Behold, you have the kingdom of God within you.

—Luke 17:20–21

Transcendence

Profoundly uplifting and transformative experiences of oneness, peace, and love are not the only results of the practice of the science of religion. Those who achieve both perfect stillness and perfect inner absorption tell us that they become aware of realities beyond the physical world. Such testimony comprises the core revelations of all religions: descriptions of heavenly worlds and angelic beings inaccessible to normal sensory perception.

Such revelations are also the most controversial aspect of religion because there would seem to be no way to validate them. But in the last 50 years or so, the efficacy of 20th-century medicine has inadvertently given us compelling validation of transcendent perception through the now ubiquitous phenomena known as near-death experiences (NDEs).

Near-death experiences were known, but rare, before the advent of highly effective emergency medical treatments. Since the mid-20th century, however, advanced practices of resuscitation and life-support have saved millions of people who might otherwise have died, resulting in a huge upsurge in the number of people who have had near-death experiences. Not everyone who has been saved from death has had a near-death experience—but an astonishing number have.

In 1982, pollster George Gallup, Jr. and author William Proctor released "Adventures in Immortality,"[13] which contains the results of extensive surveys conducted in 1980 and 1981. According to their surveys, at that time *over eight million people* in America had had a near-death experience. (Nor is the phenomenon limited to America. Researchers have found that people all over the world have had near-death experiences.)[14]

People who have had NDEs "came back to life" after their vital signs—heart, breath, and brain activity—decreased below critical levels, or ceased altogether. Most revived after a few minutes to a couple of hours. Some were in extended comas lasting for many hours to several days. A few were pronounced dead and taken to the morgue, only to revive later, causing, as you can imagine, general consternation and amazement.

Once recovered, many shared with their nurses, doctors, and loved ones extraordinary experiences they had had during their NDE. Not everyone who has had a near-death experience comes forward and publically shares his or her experience. Fearing ridicule, accusations of fraud, being considered crazy, or simply wanting to protect from cynical misinterpretation what they felt had been a sacred experience, they instead tend to keep their experiences a secret among a few trusted friends and family. However, researchers have conducted interviews with thousands of people who *have* been willing to share what they experienced; there are hundreds more who have written their own books or articles detailing their experiences. What soon impresses those who make a study of near-death experiences is the remarkable similarity and consistency of the descriptions of the experience.

Out-of-Body Experiences

Thousands of near-death experiencers describe feeling and seeing themselves floating out of, and hovering above, their physical bodies. They see their bodies on an operating table, or at the scene of an accident, as if from outside. While in that state, they can see and hear what is going on, including things that happened well outside of the range of their then-comatose body's senses. After their return to waking awareness, many accurately described conversations and activities that took place while they were "unconscious"—and many saw things that they should not have been able to see even if they had been conscious. The following are two accounts of near-death experiences. The first is from the book, *Brain Death and*

Disorders of Consciousness, as told to Dr. Pim van Lommel, Rijnstate Hospital, Netherlands by a coronary care nurse. The second is an interview of Kimberly Clark Sharp from the book, *After the Light.*

During the night shift an ambulance brings in a 44-year-old cyanotic, comatose man into the coronary care unit. He was found in coma about 30 minutes before in a meadow. When we go to intubate the patient, he turns out to have dentures in his mouth. I remove these upper dentures and put them onto the "crash cart." After about an hour and a half the patient has sufficient heart rhythm and blood pressure, but he is still ventilated and intubated, and he is still comatose. He is transferred to the intensive care unit to continue the necessary artificial respiration. Only after more than a week do I meet again with the patient, who is by now back on the cardiac ward. The moment he sees me he says: "O, that nurse knows where my dentures are." I am very surprised. Then he elucidates: "You were there when I was brought into hospital and you took my dentures out of my mouth and put them onto that cart, it had all these bottles on it and there was this sliding drawer underneath, and there you put my teeth." I was especially amazed because I remembered this happening while the man was in deep coma and in the process of CPR. It appeared that the man had seen himself lying in bed, that he had perceived from above how nurses and doctors had been busy with the CPR. He was also able to describe correctly and in detail the small room in which he had been resuscitated as well as the appearance of those present like myself. He is deeply impressed by his experience and says he is no longer afraid of death.[15]

———

Maria was a migrant worker who, while visiting friends in Seattle, had a severe heart attack. She was rushed to Harborview Hospital and placed in the coronary care unit. A few days later, she had a cardiac arrest and an unusual out-of-body experience. At one point in this experience, she found herself [floating] outside the hospital and spotted a single tennis shoe on the ledge of the north side of the third floor of the building. Maria not only was able to indicate the whereabouts of this oddly situated object, but was able to provide precise details concerning its appearance, such as that its little toe area was worn and one of its laces was stuck underneath its heel. Upon hearing Maria's story, Clark, with some considerable degree of skepticism and metaphysical misgiving, went to the location described to see whether any such shoe could be found. Indeed it was, just where and precisely as Maria had described it, except that from the window through which Clark was able to see it, the details of its appearance that Maria had specified could not be discerned. Clark concluded, "The only way she could have had such a perspective was if she had been floating right outside and at very close range to the tennis shoe. I retrieved the shoe and brought it back to Maria; it was very concrete evidence for me.[16]

Profound Peace and Well-Being

Near-death experiences are nearly always accompanied by feelings of peace and well-being so deep that the person's life is forever changed. Most say they will never fear death again. Many describe feeling the presence of an all-forgiving, all-encompassing love:

Then I simply remember I became more blissful, more rapturous, more ecstatic. I was just filling and filling with this light and love that was in the light.

—Jayne Smith, transcribed from "A Moment of Truth"[17]

A sense of all-knowing enveloped me. Every part of my being was satisfied with an unconditional love beyond description. All questions were answered. An inner peace without striving or achieving was created and understood.

—Laurelynn Martin, author of *Searching for Home*[18]

Passing Into Light

Near-death experiencers, after floating free of their bodies, frequently describe being irresistibly drawn toward a light.

Then, suddenly, I was in light; bright white, shiny and strong; a very bright light. It was like the flash of a camera, but not flickering— that bright. Constant brightness. At first I found the brilliance of the light painful, I couldn't look directly at it. But little by little I began to relax. I began to feel warm, comforted, and everything suddenly seemed fine.

—George Rodonaia, author of *The Journey Home*[19]

Arriving "in" the light, many then see a luminous reality that most describe as heaven.

Everybody there was made of light. And I was made of light. What the light conveyed was love. There was love everywhere. It was like love came from the grass, love came from the birds, love came from the trees.

—Vicki Umipeq, blind from birth[20]

I try to explain it by saying there are flashes of Light and brilliant colors of every spectrum everywhere.

—Christian Andréason, near-death experiencer[21]

The current explanation given by scientific materialists for near-death experiences is that they are nothing more than a natural extension of our ability to dream, as if, as a last gasp of consciousness, these thousands of people who experienced near death had a kind of hallucination caused by biochemical processes confined to the brain.

If that is the case, why are the accounts so similar? My dreams are hardly similar from one night to the next, let alone similar to someone else's dreams.

And how can these people know things that happened around them while they were comatose? How did Maria see a tennis shoe on the out-side third-story ledge of her hospital? How did the denture-less man know where his dentures had been placed?

And why, if NDEs are just a dream-like hallucination, does the experience leave people so deeply changed?

Although Steve was successful in reviving me, one thing was certain—the woman he had brought back was not the same one who had left. After learning that I was in essence a Being of Light, I had to come back into this world and reenter a dense, physical body. Furthermore, almost every belief I had embraced only hours before—that I was a physical being, that love was outside of me, that God was some patriarchal monarch sitting on a marble throne somewhere in the sky, that death was something to fear, that I was doomed by my past, that religion and spirituality were the same, that spirituality and science were different—was no longer true to my experience. Virtually every picture of reality I had used to define my existence—not to be confused with my life—had been cremated. The ashes of the woman I thought I was were scattered on the wind.

—Lynnclaire Dennis, author of *The Pattern*[22]

I had been alive, and aware, truly aware, in a universe characterized above all by love, consciousness, and reality. There was, for me, simply no arguing this fact. I knew it so completely that I ached.

—Eben Alexander, author of *Proof of Heaven*[23]

Although it's been 20 years since my heavenly voyage, I have never forgotten it. Nor have I, in the face of ridicule and disbelief, ever doubted its reality. Nothing that intense and life-changing could possibly have been a dream or hallucination. To the contrary, I consider the rest of my life to be a passing fantasy, a brief dream, that will end when I again awaken in the permanent presence of that giver of life and bliss.

—Beverly Brodsky, author of *Lessons From the Light*[24]

One cannot read the stories of such life-changing experiences without being moved to wonder. Open-minded researchers, including doctors and scientists, find the sincere testimony and profound life transformations of near-death experiencers impossible to dismiss as fraud or fantasy. A thorough study of near-death experiences leads any but the most determinedly skeptical to conclude that only something beyond a solely physical explanation can satisfy. These were not brain-centered, dream-like experiences drawn from an individual's random thoughts and impressions: All the near-death experiences were similar *regardless of prior beliefs*. Many of those who experienced near death were atheists. Most had no preconceived ideas about heaven or astral realms. Many who *did* have preconceptions about such transcendent realms found their actual experience to be quite *different* from their preconceptions.

One of the foundations of the scientific method is the importance of empirical, repeatable results. An experiment conducted by one scientist is not considered valid unless the experiment can be repeated by another scientist with the same results. There are clear similarities between the experiences described by those having near-death experiences and the descriptions of transcendent experiences given by enlightened saints and sages. Those who achieve perfect stillness and inner absorption—whether achieved by intention (meditation or devotion) or by accident (near-death experience)—have the same empirical results.

Since my return [from my near death experience] I have experienced the light spontaneously, and I have learned how to get to that space almost any time in my meditation. Each one of you can do this. You do not have to die to do this. It is within your equipment; you are wired for it already.

—Mellen-Thomas Benedict[25]

The consistency of the experiences of near-death experiencers is matched by the consistent revelations of enlightened saints and sages:

The astral kingdom is a realm of rainbow-hued light. Astral land, seas, skies, gardens, beings, the manifestation of day and night— all are made of variegated vibrations of light. Oceans heave with opalescent azure, green, silver, gold, red, yellow, and aquamarine. Diamond-bright waves dance in a perpetual rhythm of beauty.

—Paramhansa Yogananda, yoga master[26]

It is filled with some sort of beautiful light . . . people . . . flowers . . . angels. . . . All is filled with some indescribable joy. Heaven is a vast space, and it has a brilliant light which does not leave it.

—Vicka Ivankovic-Mijatovic, one of six children who experienced the Visions of Mary in Medjugorje, Bosnia Herzegovina[27]

I could add quote after quote after quote to the previous ones. I have read hundreds of books containing stirring accounts of near-death experiences as well as inspiring descriptions of transcendent realms given by monks, nuns, yogis, Sufis, adepts, Roshis, saints, sages, and mystics from all religions and all eras. The more one reads, the more one finds the compelling consistency I mentioned at the beginning of this chapter: Many thousands have testified that, once they have transcended the senses in perfect physical, emotional, and mental stillness, they have perceived beautifully luminous realms and angelic beings and have experienced nearly indescribable and overwhelming feelings of well-being and oneness.

This compelling consistency of the findings of saints and sages is the reason that I accord those findings as much credibility as I do the findings of science. In the chapters ahead, you will find as many quotes from saints as from scientists; you will find as many examples of religion's views as of science's views.

The primary difference between the science of religion and the science of matter is in the discovery process: the science of matter's view of reality is based on the repeatable and consistent findings of *physical experiments*; the science of religion's view of reality is based on the repeatable and consistent findings of *transcendent experience*.

As we continue our exploration, our most remarkable discovery will be that the perception of reality garnered from physical experiments and the one garnered from transcendent experience are remarkably and deeply congruent; together, they give a more complete picture of the physics of God than either can provide separately.

CHAPTER 3

The Light-Show Illusion of Matter

One example of the remarkable similarity between the findings of science and the findings of religion is that both reveal that matter is not what it seems. Many religious traditions hold that matter is an illusion; especially is this true in Hinduism, Buddhism, Jainism, and Sikhism, which embrace the concept of Maya, the veil of illusion cast over sensory perception. Yet the findings of science concur that matter is nothing like what our senses reveal. In fact, most of reality is hidden from our senses.

Our senses appear to tell us unequivocally that we live in a solid and enduring reality of matter. Those senses, however, are extremely limited. Our eyes detect only *visible* light—a very tiny portion of the electromagnetic spectrum that also includes radio waves, microwaves, infrared, ultraviolet, x-ray, and gamma waves, none of which we can perceive through our sense of sight. If our sense of sight were not limited to seeing only a narrow band of the electromagnetic spectrum, if we could "see" the rest of the spectrum, we would perceive a world entirely made up of light. Imagine there being thousands of "colors," not just the seven colors of the visible light spectrum, in a completely luminous reality.

Our ears can detect sounds that vibrate in the 20 to 20,000 Hz range. But sounds can vibrate at frequencies well beyond 20,000 Hz. Some bats can detect sounds as high as 200,000 Hz. Atoms vibrate at frequencies as high as 10,000,000,000,000 Hz. The lower range of sound, known as *infrasound*, vibrates as slowly as 0.001 Hz. Sources of such low-frequency sounds include earthquakes, volcanoes, and lightning. If our sense of hearing were not limited to our ear's narrow band of detection, we would experience a world bursting with sound—from the powerful pulses of earth movements to the continuous vibration of the atoms.

Our senses of smell, taste, and touch are similarly limited. We can smell only very specific airborne compounds, and we can taste only very specific ingested substances. Our sense of touch tells us little about what we are touching except for basic properties of texture, hardness, and temperature.

The fact is that we are mostly insensible to the world around us. It is safe to say that our senses simply cannot detect more than 99.9 percent of the wavelengths, frequencies, and vibrating substances that are actually present. If we could perceive reality fully, the picture we would have in our minds-eye would be almost completely different from the picture our senses allow us to perceive.

Matter is a light-show illusion made of vibrating energy.

Remember the diagrams of atoms in your grade-school science book? They showed a nucleus made up of protons and neutrons surrounded by circling electrons. In my sixth-grade class, we made models of the atom. We all went home and drove our parents crazy trying to help us pierce spray-painted Styrofoam balls with coat-hanger wire bent in a lumpy circle. There was one boy in my class who modeled the uranium atom. He created a massive tangle of hundreds of white, Styrofoam ball-pierced wire circles that almost completely obscured the red and blue Styrofoam ball nucleus. You may have had a boy like that in your class, too. He's probably running a tech firm now and driving to work in a Lamborghini. Let's forget him.

But do you remember the diagram? Yes? Well, forget that, too. You'll still find the diagram in modern school textbooks because it is still believed to be a useful teaching aid—but it is almost completely misleading. A truer picture of the atom, but far more difficult to visualize, has been known since the beginning of the 20th century.

The first problem with the typical school textbook diagram is the scale. A diagram of the hydrogen atom is often shown because it is the simplest—one proton in the nucleus and one orbiting electron. But if the size of the hydrogen atom's one-proton nucleus really were as big as it is depicted on the page—say, one inch in diameter—to be in proper scale, the electron would have to be drawn several miles away.

You've probably heard this old chestnut before, but it's worth repeating: If all the space between the nucleus of the atoms and their orbiting electrons were removed, our bodies would be reduced to less than the size of a pinhead. Our bodies consist nearly entirely of empty space—as in 99.9999 percent empty space.

This raises an obvious question: Why don't our bodies mesh into other objects, merging into them like two insubstantial dandelion blossoms pushed together? Or: Why do we stop so suddenly (and painfully) when our mostly-full-of-space body smacks into a mostly-full-of-space wall?

Good questions. And they bring us to the second problem with the diagram: it's static. The electron pictured as a dot in a circle around the nucleus is actually moving at the speed of light. In the time it takes to read this sentence, a single electron will have circled an atom's nucleus *trillions* of times.

Remember Fourth of July sparklers? They are illegal almost everywhere these days because they tend to set fire to things like dry grass, wooden shingles, and your uncle's patio-chair cushion. But I'm sure you've played with them. They are particularly fun at night. If you are anything like me, you whipped them through the air and saw trails of light; if you spun the tip around rapidly in a circle, there appeared to be an *actual* circle of sparkling light hovering magically in the air.

The circle of light created by twirling a sparkler isn't real. It is a result of how our eyes work and what our brain does with the information received. But the seeming reality of the circle of light is a good analogy for the effect of the electron racing around the nucleus. Moving at the speed of light, incomprehensibly faster that our twirling sparkler, the electron effectively creates a permanent shell of light energy around the nucleus. Larger atoms, with their greater number of protons and a correspondingly greater number of electrons, create what is often described as an *electron cloud* around the nucleus.

The word *cloud* suggests something soft and yielding, but in this case it is anything but. If we were inside a small space craft and somehow able to shrink it down to the size of a neutron, and then try to fly inside an atom, we would be unable to penetrate the force field of energy created by the cloud of electrons traveling around the nucleus. We'd be annihilated when our space craft took a direct hit from an electron, its impact being like a laser-cannon blast from a science-fiction spaceship.

When an atom, surrounded by its whirling electron force field, comes in contact with another atom's whirling electron force field, a number of things can happen. They can bounce off each other and go their merry ways. Or one atom can take electrons from, or give electrons to, the other atom, in a process that changes both atoms. Or they can share electrons— a sharing that effectively glues them together—thus allowing atoms to form stable arrangements of atoms known as molecules.

Everything from pancakes to planets forms from the varying inter-actions between the electron shells of atoms. One thing, however, that electron shells don't do (in ordinary conditions) is collapse. The electron force field is immensely strong. The electron force field *can* be defeated by stripping electrons away from simple atoms, such as hydrogen, leaving the proton "free." But unless carefully controlled, that proton will nearly instantaneously pick up an electron from some other obliging atom and the force field will form once more.

It is this force field–like electron cloud around every atom that keeps our mostly-full-of-space body from meshing into other mostly-full-of-space objects—or from sinking into the ground on which we stand. A helpful visual analogy is that a large cardboard box tightly packed with Ping Pong balls, all of which are hollow, would easily hold your weight if you stood on it. Similarly, the ground easily supports your weight even though our solid-seeming earth is 99.9999 percent space.

Now for the last problem with our grade school diagram: That dot in the center of the diagram that represents the nucleus? It isn't matter either! Like the force-field electron shell of constantly moving energy that surrounds the protons and neutrons of the nucleus, protons and neutrons are *also* composed of energy moving at the speed of light.

Einstein was the first scientist to make the case mathematically that matter as it had been understood simply doesn't exist. In 1905, Einstein published a paper describing his Special Theory of Relativity, in which he declared that the nucleus of the atom was actually a super-condensed, super-high frequency form of energy. His famous equation, $E = mc^2$, proved that there are no undividable, super-tiny little balls of solidity.

The absence of "solid" matter at the core of the atom has since been proven over and over in particle-accelerator experiments. In ordinary conditions, the electron cloud around the nucleus prevents other forms of light energy from penetrating to the nucleus, thus preventing scientists from "seeing" through to the nucleus. The situation is roughly analogous to not being able to see inside an egg because of the shell. Stymied by this opacity, pioneering physicists reasoned that if they couldn't see into the atom, they could smash the atom to bits and then examine the pieces, rather like smashing an egg and examining the contents.

In 1929, Ernest O. Lawrence of the University of California, Berkeley, invented the first "atom smasher," or particle accelerator, as it is known today. Lawrence's atom smasher is the many-greats grandfather of the Large Hadron Collider (LHC) built at CERN in Switzerland. What has subsequently been revealed is nothing like our science book's simple diagram of the atom.

I won't even begin to try to describe to you a complete picture of what has become known as the Standard Model of the atom. Most people are quickly snowed under by the blizzard of terms used in the Standard Model to describe the ever smaller and ever more exotic subatomic particles that have been created and identified in particle accelerator experiments—quarks, bosons, hadrons, fermions, photons, gluons, mesons, baryons, leptons, muons, pions, kaons—and these are just a few flakes in the avalanche of Standard Model terms that will bury the unwary.

Fortunately, stepping back from the model's avalanche of detail will not only save us from an icy burial, it will also provide us the key insight into the Standard Model. The LHC is able to accelerate a stream of protons (atoms stripped of their electrons) up to very high speeds and then collide it with another stream of protons coming from the opposite direction, like two cars in a head-on smash. For an inconceivably tiny moment of time after the collision (we're talking trillionths of a second), stable particles (such as quarks) become unstable and then reform into multiple new particles, rather like a few drops of water instantly superheated into gas inside a chamber and then just as instantly cooled back into droplets.

However, unlike the superheated water droplets, the enormous amount of energy used to speed the proton streams to near light speeds is *also* converted into particles at the moment of collision. Because more energy has been added to the mix, the protons do not reform exactly into their original state; the additional energy upsets the intricate and stable balance of forces composing the original protons. One way to think of this process is that by adding more energy, scientists are creating *new* kinds of particles.

What these particle-accelerator experiments have revealed is that the nucleus of the atom is essentially a dynamic vibrating balance of high-energy forces, which, when new forces are introduced, loses equilibrium and seeks a new balance. The Standard Model is often described as a theory of *fundamental interactions*, as opposed to a theory of fundamental particles. None of the "particles" (in the avalanche of terms to which I have subjected you) can exist on its own. All these particles exist only when in dynamic balance with other forces and particles. Furthermore, some of the particles (some bosons for example), are not, strictly speaking, particles at all, because they have no mass; instead, they serve to "carry" forces between particles that do have mass.

Taking even further the idea that matter is only energies in a stable vibrating equilibrium is the theory that a particle is really just an *excited* state of an underlying *field*. This approach is generally known as field theory (FT), but it becomes known as quantum field theory (QFT) when the behavior of such fields is considered at the subatomic level. Instead of having to visualize a collided particle vaporizing into an unstable fog of energy and then recondensing into a new and stable form, imagine instead that there is no particle—there never was; instead, the added energies have caused new excitations at different points in a field.

Hard to visualize, I know. But keep in mind that even with all the amazing tools of discovery used to explore the atom and the subatomic realms, scientists have never been able to "see" any of the particles they theorize about; they can only *deduce* their presence and properties from experimental data. In the particle-collider world, the results of the experimental collisions are captured by detectors sensitive to high-energy radiation and electromagnetic energy. These detectors provide spectacular images of what looks to the uneducated eye like an explosion. What the detectors detect are quanta (energy packets) hitting the detectors in the instants after the collision (Figure 7).

It is fair, then, to ask: Are those quanta emitted from a particle or from the vibration of a field? At the instant of collision, did a particle momentarily become formless energy and then reform as another type of particle, or was it energy all along? And does it make any difference? The answer to the last question is: Not really. Einstein's discovery of the equivalence of matter and energy renders the question irrelevant.

As I mentioned previously, "particles" called bosons, specifically photons and gluons, have no mass at all. Even particles *with* mass, such as quarks, have their mass quantified as the electronvolts of *energy* they contain. The desire to classify the subatomic realm in terms of particles is purely a reflection of the way we think about the everyday world as our

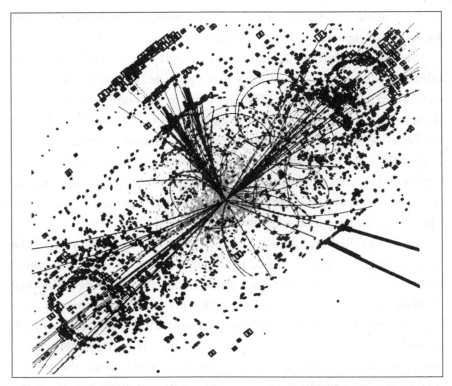

FIGURE 7. *A computer-generated image showing the creation of a Higgs boson at the Large Hadron Collider (LHC) at CERN in Switzerland. Photo credit: Creative Commons, CERN,* http://cdsweb.cern.ch/record/628469.

senses reveal it. We deal with discrete objects. We pick up a glass. We throw a ball. We clean a fork. We are predisposed to visualize the sub-atomic realm in a similar way—but it simply isn't similar.

I mentioned "mass" in a previous paragraph. It may surprise you to know that until the recent confirmation of the existence of the now-famous Higgs boson, physicists had *no* proven way to explain why *any* particle, whether considered as matter or considered as energy, would have more mass than any other particle.

In everyday terms, mass can be understood to mean the weight of an object. We understand that a one-centimeter cube of gold weighs more than a one-centimeter cube of carbon. But weight is relative to gravity. A one-centimeter cube of gold on the moon weighs less—using the same kind of measuring device—than a one-centimeter cube of carbon does on Earth, because the gravity on the moon is one sixth that of Earth's.

Scientists, therefore, came up with a way of measuring mass that is independent of gravity: The measure of mass became *a body's resistance to being accelerated by a force*. For example, if you had a one-meter cube of gold and a one-meter cube of carbon floating in space—where there is no gravity and no air resistance—in addition to not having to worry about your retirement, you would have to apply more force to accelerate the cube of gold to, say, one kilometer per hour, than you would have to apply to accelerate the one-meter cube of carbon to one kilometer per hour, thus demonstrating the greater mass of gold than carbon.

But why? Despite this gravity-independent way of determining the mass of an object, particle physicists were hard-pressed to explain why the vibrating energy that forms into the stable pattern of gold should have more resistance to being accelerated by a force than the vibrating energy that forms into the stable pattern of carbon. Both gold and carbon are simply energy!

Enter the Higgs boson and, more importantly for our discussion, the *Higgs field*. The recent trillionth-of-a-second appearances of the Higgs boson in the LHC's detectors not only added one more confirmed species to the many exotic species in the particle accelerator zoo, it also, and more importantly, confirmed for physicists the existence of the Higgs field.

The Higgs field is theorized to permeate *all of space* and is believed to be what imparts mass to all particles. Subatomic particles moving through the Higgs field have been compared to everyday objects moving through molasses. The larger the object the harder it is to move it through the molasses. Similarly, higher-energy particles (which have a correspondingly higher mass) interact more with the Higgs field than do lower-energy particles, and therefore require more force to move through the field.

Why is the Higgs field important for us to understand? Because it demonstrates that even mass—weight, in terrestrial terms—the property that appears to give one object more "substance" than another, is simply due to the interactions of the atom's energy with the energy of an invisible field: energies interacting with energies.

Everything we perceive, from the seemingly solid world around us to the very sensation of weight, is energy. Matter is, genuinely, a light-show illusion. By *illusion*, I don't mean that it isn't there; rather, I mean that it isn't what is seems. We know that a movie is an illusion, but we wouldn't say that it isn't there—it just isn't what it seems. If we are watching a movie in a theater, beams of light reflect off the screen and excite our eye's rods and cones, and artificially created sound waves vibrate our ear drums. Together, they create the illusion in our mind's eye of a "real" world. The physical world we interact with every day only seems more real to us than a movie because all five of our senses, not just sight and hearing, are engaged with the illusion we call the physical world.

The visible world is the invisible organization of energy.
—Heinz Pagels, former executive director,
New York Academy of Sciences[1]

The seemingly solid and substantial physical world around us is an amazing, invisibly organized, light-show illusion—an intricate dance of vibrating energy—far different from what our senses reveal, far less substantial than we experience, far more evanescent than we believe.

Beneath matter's seeming solidity is a fluid dance of energy. Matter's essential fluidity gives us the first hint of how miracles and other phenomena, such as telekinesis, can occur: That matter results from the "invisible organization of energy" suggests the possibility that this invisible organization can be changed. Matter is not fixed; it is not a permanently unchanging *thing*. (There is much more on this subject ahead.)

Next, we'll explore another view of reality shared by religion and science: The physical universe, as astonishingly big as it is, is a relatively tiny part of the cosmos. There is much more to reality than the three-dimensional realm of matter familiar to us. Physicists have for decades theorized that there must exist a two-dimensional realm of pure energy that is inconceivably vaster than our physical universe. And this realm of pure energy has long been understood by saints and sages to be the true location of the heavens described by every religion.

CHAPTER 4

The Energy-verse and the Heavens

Over the span of the 20th and now the 21st centuries, branches of physics have produced an astonishingly vast and predominantly nonmaterial view of the cosmos, a cosmos of which our enormous physical universe is only a tiny part. Current theories in physics, quantum theory, and, especially, string theory relegate our physical universe—which, as we just explored, is essentially organized energy held in stable patterns—to be a small, self-contained, three-dimensional energy "bubble" in a virtually infinite two-dimensional ocean of energy—what I like to call the *energy-verse*.

Physicists are not alone in describing a much larger, nonmaterial cosmos beyond the physical universe. Saints, sages, and near-death experiencers have also described heavenly worlds of pure energy: luminous, nonphysical realms that permeate our physical universe.

The saints and sages arrived at this view through transcendent experience. Physicists arrived at this view because they have been forced to conclude, for a variety of reasons, that the measurable matter and energy in our universe cannot fully explain why the universe behaves as it does. Any mathematical model that includes only the universe's visible matter and measurable energy in its equations simply doesn't "add up" to the actual behavior of the universe.

In the early part of the 20th century, while developing his theories of gravity (General Relativity), Einstein struggled to explain why gravity's combined strength throughout the universe (as a result of the combined gravitational effect of all the matter in the universe) isn't making the universe contract. Einstein's equations, which took into account only the gravitational effects of the observed matter in the universe, suggested that the universe should be contracting rapidly and, additionally, that it never should have expanded to its present size in the first place—or even have formed at all.

In order to get his equations to match up to reality, Einstein put forward the idea that there is a *cosmological constant*, a constant level of undetected background energy present in the universe that counteracts matter's combined force of gravity. The original mathematical value he chose for the cosmological constant, when inserted into his equations of general relativity, maintains the universe in a static state—neither contracting nor expanding.

When subsequent discoveries by Edwin Hubble (1889–1953) showed that the universe was, in fact, *expanding*, Einstein called the idea of a cosmological constant his greatest blunder, because he made an incorrect assumption that the universe was static. Blunder or not, and whatever the proper value of the cosmological constant should be to account for what we now know to be an expanding universe, the notion that the universe contains more energy than can be currently measured remains a requirement in the equations of general relativity—without it, the equations of general relativity do not match up to the measured behavior of the universe.

Later in the 20th century, quantum physicists also posited, for different reasons than Einstein's, that the universe must have a significant, ever-present but undetectable background energy. Quantum physicists theorize that the background energy—sometimes called *vacuum energy* or *zero-point energy*—exists in a quantum *energy field* that is present throughout all of space. Unlike the more familiar magnetic field, which weakens with distance from its source, the quantum energy field is thought to be equally potent everywhere in the universe.

The quantum energy field is theorized to be quite active. Quantum physicists think that pairs of oppositely charged virtual particles constantly wink into being in the midst of space and then annihilate each other in a time span too short to be measured. This concept led Princeton professor John Archibald Wheeler (1911–2008), an eminent theoretical physicist and collaborator with Einstein, to poetically describe this ceaseless activity as *quantum foam*. Where matter is present, such as we experience living on planet Earth, it is the restless quantum energy field that is continuously giving rise to matter.

There is yet another argument for the presence of undetected energy in the universe. In addition to the cosmological constant and the notion of an omnipresent quantum field, in the 1990s the need for *dark energy* was thrust upon physicists by the unexpected discovery that the universe is expanding at an accelerating rate. Previous values for the cosmological constant, and concepts of how the cosmological constant actually worked, turned out to be significantly inadequate to explain how the universe's rate of expansion could be *accelerating*. Simply increasing the value of the cosmological constant could not get relativity's equations to match this newly measured reality.

Deeper research into the accelerating expansion of the universe has led to the startling discovery that *all of the detectable matter in the universe* accounts for only 4.9 percent of the gravity! Physicists had to posit two new theories to account for the remaining 95.1 percent of gravity: *dark matter* and *dark energy*. It is speculated that dark matter forms a (so far) undetectable halo-like cloud around galaxies and is theorized to account for 26.8 percent of the gravity in the universe. Dark energy, also so far undetected, is posited to be a type of energy with properties unlike any energy currently known—a type of energy that expands space and pushes matter apart—and accounts in current estimations for an astonishing 68.3 percent of the observed gravitational effect in the universe.

Added to these other arguments for the presence of more energy in the universe than can be measured is *string theory*. String theory, which made its debut in the mid-20th century, posits that there is a vast, unseen, all-pervading realm that interpenetrates the physical universe at every point. This unseen realm is thought to be filled with tiny, vibrating two-dimensional rings and strings of pure energy that vibrate at wavelengths far, far smaller than those measurable with our physical instruments; these rings and strings are thought to be as much smaller than the nucleus of an atom as the nucleus of an atom is smaller than the human body! String theory posits that *everything* in the universe arises from this two-dimensional ocean of infinitesimally small rings and strings of vibrating energy—forming all matter, all measurable energy, all gravity—even space itself.

All of these theories—relativity's cosmological constant, quantum physics' quantum foam, cosmological physics' dark energy, and string theory's vibrating rings and strings—suggest that the universe is suffused with energies that significantly influence how the universe works. As you can appreciate by dark energy's outsized role at 68.3 percent of the gravitational effect found in the universe, and string theory's assertion that *everything* is the result of unseen vibrating rings and strings of energy, these theories suggest that energy is far more significant in the creation and continuous presence of the universe than is matter. The physical universe, and all the matter it contains, is increasingly understood to be a *small by-product* of the interactions of the far more vast energy-verse. String theory's conception of the energy-verse is so vast that it has room for millions upon millions of more three-dimensional energy-bubble universes! Our universe could be one of many others.

Of all the branches of physics that posit the energy-verse, the one that deals with it most centrally is string theory. What led to the advent of string theory is mathematics; more accurately put, *problems* with mathematics is what led to the advent of string theory. String theory is an attempt to solve an enduring and troubling mystery: Two of the most important mathematical systems in physics—general relativity and quantum theory—are, mathematically, deeply incompatible.

This incompatibility is a big problem. To have the two most important branches of physics be mathematically incompatible is like having two major world languages—say, Chinese and English—be untranslatable one to the other.

Physics *depends* on mathematics—for research, exploration, and theoretical confirmation. Mathematics is the universal language of physics. It remains a mystery to scientists why mathematics has the ability to so accurately describe the structure and behaviors of reality, but it is impossible to be a physicist and not have come to appreciate that it does. This conformance of mathematics and reality inspires many physicists, even avowed atheists, to near-mystical speculation:

> The miracle of the appropriateness of the language of mathematics for the formulation of the laws of physics is a wonderful gift which we neither understand nor deserve.
> —Eugene Wigner, Noble Prize–winning physicist[1]

> One cannot escape the feeling that these mathematical formulas have an independent existence and an intelligence of their own, that they are wiser than we are, wiser even than their discoverers.
> —Heinrich Hertz, first to prove the existence
> of electromagnetic waves[2]

> One could perhaps describe the situation by saying that God is a mathematician of a very high order, and He used very advanced mathematics in constructing the universe.
> —Paul Dirac, Nobel Prize–winning physicist
> and mathematician[3]

Little wonder that physicists are so perplexed and concerned that physics' two central systems—general relativity and quantum physics—have resisted all attempts at mathematical integration.

General relativity theory, pioneered by Einstein, among others, has ramified into equations that fill hundreds of volumes. The equations of relativity have their most useful application on large astronomical scales and are successfully used to understand "real world" outcomes from the Big Bang to black holes. Similarly, quantum theory, pioneered by Max Planck and Neils Bohr, among others, has also ramified into equations that fill hundreds of volumes. The equations of quantum theory have their most useful application on tiny, subatomic scales and are successfully used to explain "real world" outcomes from nuclear reactions to interactions in particle colliders.

When quantum physicists try to use their system of equations to explain gravity, for example, their equations tell them that gravity should be many times stronger than the observed reality. Similarly, when the equations of general relativity are applied to subatomic phenomena, the equations give impossible answers that do not even remotely conform to any observed reality.

String theory seeks to solve the problem of integrating these two systems by developing a deeper math that underlies them both, somewhat analogous to finding a solution to my hypothetical language problem by creating a third language that can be translated into both Chinese and English, thus creating a bridge from one to the other.

One of the many incompatibilities between the equations of general relativity and quantum theory, and one that string theory solves, is the huge discrepancy in calculations to determine how much energy exists in space. Using relativity's equations, physicists have predicted that there are 10^{-9} joules (a *joule* is a unit of energy) in one cubic meter of space.[4] Using quantum mechanics' equations, physicists have predicted that there are 10^{113} joules of energy in one cubic meter of space.[5] Quite a difference—the two predictions differ by an order of magnitude of 122!

Not even government contractors can get away with that.

If quantum physics' prediction of the higher amount of energy is correct, we should see the universe behave much differently than general

74

relativity predicts; but, in fact, the universe behaves as if general relativity's prediction of the lower amount of energy in space is true. Yet if quantum theory's prediction that vastly more energy exists in the fabric of space than general relativity can account for is correct—and there really are very few doubters that it *is* correct—then that energy has to be *somewhere*.

M-theory, string theory's most accepted version, attempts to reconcile the difference between the two calculations by positing that the higher energy predicted by quantum theory does indeed exist somewhere else: It exists in *extra dimensions* beyond the four dimensions with which general relativity concerns itself (three dimensions of space and one of time) and beyond our senses' and our finest instruments' ability to detect. In this theory, the three dimensions of our already almost incomprehensibly large physical universe are the *smallest* dimensions in the cosmos!

In M-theory, all dimensions exist in what are called *branes*. "Brane" is an odd word easily confused with "brain." Physicists, however, have gotten used to it, and so must we. The word is a contraction of membrane and is used to suggest a barrier or boundary that divides or encloses, keeping the contents of one region separate from other regions. M-theory posits that there are relatively small branes that are *three-dimensional*, such as our universe, and other super-large regions that are *two-dimensional*—all of which make up the *brane-world*—what we would more familiarly call the *cosmos*.

More on the nature of the two-dimensional branes in a moment, but first let's explore what M-theory has to say about the three-dimensional brane we know as our universe.

In M-theory, there is a specialized class of three-dimensional branes called *D-branes*. A D-brane's properties make it a self-contained three-dimensional region; it is self-contained because it is impossible to *travel* outside of a D-brane as well as impossible to *observe* anything outside of a D-brane. Thus M-theorists say that we are "stuck" in our D-brane universe. Put another way, the properties of a three-dimensional D-brane mean that we can never travel in spaceships to other branes nor detect other branes with physical instruments that rely on electromagnetic energy such as visible light. It is as if the universe were a house of mirrors: When we try to see what's without, we can only see a reflection of what's within.

Relativity's mind-bending laws explain how a D-brane works.

One of the laws of relativity that bends the mind is that our universe has no edge. If someone began a billions-of-years journey in a spaceship that could travel at near-light speeds—assuming he could live for billions of years and had plenty of reading material to while away the millennia—even if he stayed on a single, straight-line course away from Earth, he would *never* reach an edge. The reason is that *gravity curves* space, and the combined gravity in our universe warps the universe into a "shape" that defies visualization. As our traveler made his way through the complete works of Shakespeare (for the 10-millionth time), thinking all the while that he had been going in a straight line for billions of years, he would have in fact been moving along a curved path, a path that will never allow him to find an edge.

Perhaps even more mind-bending is that, as our well-read traveler journeyed, wherever he was in the universe, *it always appeared to him that he was in the center*. No matter where he was, everything else appeared to be moving away from him, as if his location were the starting point of an explosion. This is because space is expanding *everywhere at once*. The distance between all the stars is constantly increasing, like dots on a balloon that get farther apart as the balloon is inflated.

Although space inexorably expands, in one human lifetime the distances to our nearby stars do not change significantly. If there were a star one light year away from Earth, and another star two light years away from Earth, the second star would have moved twice as far away from Earth in, say, one year as the first star would have moved, but it would still not be noticeable except to finely calibrated instruments. However, a star a thousand light years away from Earth would have moved a thousand times farther away in the same amount of time. When you consider a star that is billions of light years away from us, that star is effectively rocketing away from us billions of times faster than are our nearby stars. The uniform expansion of space therefore gives us the impression that no matter where we are in the universe, we are at the center, because all the stars—in every direction we observe—are moving away from us.

The impression that you are in the center of the universe is further reinforced by the fact that the most distant objects you see, no matter where you are in the universe, will always appear to be the oldest. The most distant objects appear to be the oldest because the light coming from those stars left them the longest time ago. If, however, we could instantaneously travel to one of those "oldest" stars, our impression would be reversed; that is, the most distant objects—where we had instantaneously traveled *from*—would *now* appear to be the oldest.

Space curves; the universe has no edge. No matter where one is in the universe, one will appear to be the center; and the most distant objects will always be moving away from one the fastest. Relativity's implications will make your head hurt if you try to visualize them. This is because our three-dimensional, energy-bubble, D-brane universe is a light-show illusion, profoundly and confoundingly shaped by the underlying, two-dimensional energy-verse that creates and sustains it.

The D-brane is derived from M-theory's mathematical model that incorporates the laws of relativity; relativity's space-time continuum, with all its mind-bending qualities, is string theory's D-brane. But according to M-theory, in order for our self-contained, three-dimensional, D-brane, energy-bubble universe to exist, and to behave the way it does within the overall mathematics of string theory, there must be other, super-large, *two-dimensional* branes of pure energy zillions of times larger than the physical universe.

Depending on the mathematical assumptions being made, the number of super-large, two-dimensional branes posited by string theorists varies from *brane world scenario* to *brane world scenario*. In M-theory, the number of super-large branes is typically seven. Collectively, physicists call all these extra, super-large dimensions the *bulk*—as in "the bulk of the cosmos."

(M-theory's term *bulk* corresponds to my term *energy-verse*. "Bulk" is an awkward word that conveys little about its actual qualities—especially that it is made up of energy. Given the pace of change in physics, as theories are refined or new discoveries are made, names such as *bulk* may come and go. *Energy-verse* is a more general term, but consistent with the direction of the discoveries made in the 20th, and now 21st, centuries.)

Although imperceptible to our senses or even to our most sensitive scientific instruments, the energy-verse's high-frequency energies *interpenetrate* our D-brane universe at every point. Although our D-brane, bubble-universe's three-dimensionality is self-contained—we can't travel out of it or see out of it—the two-dimensional energies of the energy-verse suffuse it like water in a sponge.

Although we cannot measure the high-frequency energies of the energy-verse because their wavelengths are too small for us to detect, quantum physicists and string theorists are certain that, if these high-frequency energies were not present, the universe would simply vanish. Every atom in the universe—even space itself—depends on the high-frequency energy-verse to exist.

The part of the energy-verse that interpenetrates our universe is Heisenberg's mysterious realm of Potentia, the source of Wigner's *quantum foam*, out of which matter winks into being, and string theory's ocean of rings and strings from which all matter and space are formed. One can also readily make the connection that the high-frequency energy of the energy-verse is the source of the background energy of Einstein's cosmological constant and provides dark energy's 68 percent contribution to the gravitational effect in the universe.

The energy-verse is also, I believe, the location of the heavens of all religious traditions; where we live after death; where angelic beings dwell. The essential qualities of the energy-verse—that it is nearly infinite, that it exists "beyond" the physical universe, and that it contains only non-material, two-dimensional, high-frequency vibrating energy, matches uncannily well the descriptions of the heavens, or luminous *astral* regions, given by hundreds of saints, sages, and near-death experiencers.

Your first reaction to the possibility of life in a two-dimensional world might be puzzled disbelief that life in a two-dimensional world would be even remotely desirable—let alone heavenly. It's easy to picture oneself squashed flat and unable to move, like a deuce in a deck of cards! Our familiarity with space's three-dimensionality instinctively makes us feel that a two-dimensional existence would not only be undesirable but downright impossible.

However, the key point to remember is that life in a two-dimensional brane would be composed of pure energy. The descriptions of heaven shared by saints, sages, and near-death experiencers suggest that heaven is *like* our physical world, but finer, nonmaterial, and unconstrained by the limitations of space, time, and matter:

> Just as persons on the cinema screen appear to move and act through a series of light pictures, and do not actually breathe, so the astral beings walk and work as intelligently guided and coordinated images of light.
>
> —Sri Yukteswar, yoga master[6]

> Heaven is a world much like our own except there is no time nor space as we think of them here. Heaven exists in a higher dimension of energy. The higher realms are a world of inexpressible beauty.
>
> —Nora Spurgin, near-death experiencer and researcher[7]

> The astral universe, made of various subtle vibrations of light and color, is hundreds of times larger than the material cosmos.
>
> —Sri Yukteswar, yoga master[8]

> Time as I had known it came to a halt; past, present, and future were somehow fused together for me in the timeless unity of life.

I learned that all the physical rules for human life were nothing when compared to this unitive reality.

—George Rodonaia, near-death experiencer[9]

C.G. Jung (1875–1961) wrote in his autobiographical *Memories, Dreams, Reflections* descriptions of near-death experiences he had in 1944 while in a hospital as the result of a heart attack. During his near death he experienced profound freedom and ecstasy. For several weeks after his initial experience, while still in hospital convalescence, he had blissfully transcendent visions during the night and difficulty reintegrating with his physical body during the day:

> It is impossible to convey the beauty and intensity of emotion during those visions. They were the most tremendous things I have ever experienced. And what a contrast the day was: I was tormented and on edge; everything irritated me; everything was too material, too crude and clumsy, terribly limited both spatially and spiritually. It was all an imprisonment, for reasons impossible to divine, and yet it had a kind of hypnotic power, a cogency, as if it were reality itself, for all that I had clearly perceived its emptiness. Although my belief in the world returned to me, I have never since entirely freed myself of the impression that . . . this life is a segment of existence which is enacted in a three-dimensional box-like universe especially set up for it.[10]

I could go on. The literature of near-death experiencers and the transcendent experiences of the spiritually awakened is full of such descriptions. Far from being an undesirable, unnatural state, the heavens or astral regions are glowingly and consistently described as surpassingly beautiful, surpassingly finer versions of the world we know. Time does not flow as we experience it. Movement is not governed by Newton's laws of motion or by Einstein's speed of light. The reality of heaven is far more subtle, flexible, and mutable than our physical existence, yet it feels unquestionably real—most witnesses say it feels much *more* real than our physical world.

Not only are the qualities of two-dimensional branes congruent with descriptions of the heavens or astral regions, there is another aspect of brane theory that aligns with descriptions of the heavens: their layered structure. Each brane, as mathematically conjectured by string physicists, has a unique set of properties and conditions, ones necessary to make the combined effects of *all* the branes "add up" to the observed behaviors of space, time, and matter in our three-dimensional, D-brane universe.

The bulk has sometimes been described by string physicists as a loaf of bread cut into individual brane "slices"—each with its own properties. (If every brane had the same properties and boundary conditions as the others, there would be no need for separate branes.) One significant property physicists must determine for each brane slice of the bulk loaf is its energy density, that is, the frequencies or wavelengths of the energies contained in the brane. It can be said that, in these various brane-world scenarios, branes *vibrate* at successively higher frequencies. This frequency structure matches, again uncannily well, the descriptions of multiple layers, levels, or realms of heaven given by enlightened saints and sages as well as near-death experiencers.

In the Christian tradition we find many biblical references to multiple heavens:

In My Father's house are many dwelling places; if it were not so, I would have told you; for I go to prepare a place for you.

—John 14:2

I know a man in Christ who fourteen years ago was caught up to the third heaven. Whether it was in the body or out of the body I do not know.

—2 Cor. 12:2-4

But who is able to build a temple for him, since the heavens, even the highest heavens, cannot contain him?

—2 Chron. 2:6

In Judaism there is a long tradition of mysticism contained in the teachings of the Kabbalah. The transcendent experiences described in the Kabbalah by its practitioners include visits to 10 subtle angelic realms, which exist within the 10 emanations of Light that continuously create both the physical realm and a chain of higher realms. The 10 emanations of Light are known collectively as *Sephirot*. Each emanation of light is described as being progressively more refined, higher, and more subtle.

One of the highest holy days of the Muslim calendar, *Lailat al Mi'raj*, celebrates Mohammed's journey through seven heavens, as described in the Hadith. Mohammed is taken, while his body sleeps, through seven increasingly more exalted realms, each with its own qualities and purpose.

The Buddhists, including Zen and Tibetan Buddhists, similarly hold a belief in a hierarchy of realms. Some traditions have 10 realms—our physical realm, plus many more heavenly realms through which souls move between incarnations as they work out their karma. Hinduism's heavenly descriptions contain a hierarchy of seven realms or *lokas*, each more subtle than the last, beginning with *Bhuva Loka*, the physical world, and ending with *Satya Loka*, the highest heaven.

Such conceptions of the heavens are also confirmed by near-death experiencers:

There are many different Heavens. . . . They are stacked one atop the other like pancakes and scattered all throughout God's super Universe.

—Christian Andréason, near-death experiencer[11]

These various descriptions of heaven are consistent with string theory's various brane-world scenarios in which we find the bulk "sliced" into two-dimensional branes with differing properties and varying frequencies of energy. Physicists themselves are not above speculating on what sentient life would be like in such conditions: For the 2014 movie *Interstellar*, prominent string theorist Kip Thorne helped shape the idea of "bulk beings" living in higher dimensional realms.

Most people, understandably, equate life with having physical bodies and equate reality with what the physical body's senses can reveal. But if, as the enlightened saints and sages of all religions agree, a more subtle essence of ourselves lives on after death, then it suggests not only that we will live in another realm but that we will live in it *without* a physical body.

> But if prophets down the millenniums spake with truth, man is essentially of incorporeal nature. [Man] is only temporarily allied with sense perception.
>
> —Parmahansa Yogananda, yoga master[12]

Even though the energy-verse's high-frequency energies are undetectable to physical instruments, the mathematics of M-theory tells us that they permeate the physical universe. The interpenetrating energy-verse is the realm of Potentia from which all matter springs, the cause of quantum foam, and the source of dark energy and the vibrating rings and strings that make up all matter—as well as space itself. The mathematics of string theory tells us that the energy-verse sustains the three-dimensional physical universe: Were the energy-verse to cease to exist, the physical universe would vanish in an instant.

Our universe is like an air-filled bubble in an ocean of water. The Big Bang is the moment that our D-brane bubble universe "pops" into being and begins to inflate with space, time, and matter. Our light-show illusion universe is a space-filled, three-dimensional, lower-frequency energy bubble in a two-dimensional ocean of higher-frequency energy.

Not only is the light-show illusion universe not what it seems, it is but a small part of a much larger cosmos. We are unable to directly detect the larger cosmos because relativity's laws, like the shiny and reflective surface of a soap bubble seen from the inside, only show us the reflection of what's within our bubble-universe.

Fortunately, however, the saints, sages, and near-death experiencers are not limited by the senses and by relativity's laws, and can transcend the house-of-mirrors bubble. They describe experientially what physicists derive mathematically. In transcendence they see string theory's brane-slices of the bulk-loaf as many layers of heaven suited to the unique vibration of each one who arrives there after death.

The transcendent experience is that life in a two-dimensional pure-energy realm is far from impossible, and very far from undesirable, that it is in fact more true to *what we really are* than the physical world can ever be. Their experience is of soaring, joyous freedom from the limitations of three-dimensional solidity and blissful absorption in harmonious, luminously beautiful worlds.

CHAPTER 5

Heaven Is a Hologram

According to many enlightened saints, sages, and near-death experiencers, the heavens are not only our afterlife destination, they also embody the *ideal form* of the physical universe. From firsthand experience, such people testify that the heavens contain a *perfect* template of what is only *imperfectly* manifested as the physical universe.

The brilliant polymath and Christian mystic, Emanuel Swedenborg (1688–1772), for many years had transcendent and transformative experiences of the heavens. Of particular interest in light of this book, Swedenborg began his life in Sweden as a scientist and inventor. He pioneered many new directions in geometry, chemistry, metallurgy, anatomy, and physiology, and was widely acknowledged as a scientific genius. At age 52, he turned his inquisitive mind to more subtle realities. His researches led to numerous transcendent experiences lasting over a period of almost 30 years. One of his findings was that the heavens provide a template for the natural world; he refers to the connection between heaven and earth as a "correspondence": "In a word, absolutely everything in nature, from the smallest to the greatest, is a correspondence. The reason correspondences occur is that the natural world, including everything in it, arises and is sustained from the spiritual world, and both worlds come from the Divine.[1]

In Eastern religions we find the concept of astral worlds:

Just as many physical suns and stars roam in space, so there are also countless astral solar and stellar systems. The astral world is infinitely beautiful, clean, pure, and orderly.

—Sri Yukteswar, yoga master[2]

The blueprints of everything in the physical universe have been astrally conceived—all the forms and forces in nature, including the complex human body, have been first produced in that realm where God's causal ideations are made visible in forms of heavenly light and vibratory energy.

—Paramhansa Yogananda, yoga master[3]

In the testimony of near-death experiencers we find similar descriptions:

Everything was created of spirit matter before it was created physically—solar systems, suns, moons, stars, planets, life upon the planets, mountains, rivers, seas, etc. I saw this process, and then, to further understand it, I was told . . . that the spirit creation could be compared to one of our photographic prints; the spirit creation would be like a sharp, brilliant print, and the Earth would be like its dark negative. This Earth is only a shadow of the beauty and glory of its spirit creation.

—Betty J. Eadie, author of *Embraced by the Light*[4]

Although many physicists are likely to be highly skeptical of the transcendent revelations of those previously quoted, and would probably deny that any heavenly template is required to explain why the physical universe formed as it did, few physicists would deny that we live in a universe that is perfectly created for the existence of intelligent life. It is so perfect that it is sometimes called the *Goldilocks universe*. As in the fairy tale, our universe is "just right."

Alter any one value and the universe could not exist . . . the odds against the universe existing are so heart-stoppingly astronomical that the notion that it all "just happened" defies common sense. It would be like tossing a coin and having it come up heads 10 quintillion times in a row. Really?

—Eric Metaxas, author of *Miracles: What They Are, Why They Happen, and How They Can Change Your Life*[5]

Clearly, the odds against our universe forming precisely as it has, combined with the odds against intelligent life emerging from inert matter once the universe did form as it has, are stunningly high. Yet, despite the relatively new and building evidence for how precisely tuned the conditions of creation have to be to produce intelligent life, many scientists still believe that absolutely everything in creation is the ultimate result of a long string of purely random events—from the birth of the universe, to the first single-cell organism, to Shakespeare's plays.

Randomness versus order is one of the most central divides between science and religion. A central tenet of religion is that the cosmos was created by an intelligent Creator. Scientific materialists on the other hand, seeing no direct evidence of such a colossal intelligence in the interactions of energy and matter, insist that the cosmos must have formed as it did accidentally in an eons' long series of random events.

Although randomness versus order is a well-known divide between religion and science, less well known is that the same divide between randomness and order can be found *within* science itself: Not all scientists nor scientific theories embrace randomness. On one side of the divide are those scientists who believe that reality is indeterminate and formed as it did randomly. On the other side of the divide are those scientists who believe that reality is determinate and formed as it did in conformance with a *hidden order.*

These two fundamentally different scientific points of view—indeterminate randomness versus determination by a hidden order—can be most clearly seen in what are called the *interpretations* of quantum physics. There are roughly a dozen interpretations of quantum physics altogether, and they are split about 50/50 along the lines of indeterminism and determinism.

In general, each interpretation of quantum physics offers a different explanation for the various counterintuitive findings of quantum physics—popularly known as *quantum weirdness*. There are three scientific discoveries that provide the best illustrations of quantum weirdness: wave-particle duality, the uncertainty principle, and the intelligent-observer paradox.

Wave-Particle Duality

Quantum physics' first counterintuitive discovery was nature's Jekyll-Hyde behavior: Energy can behave like matter and matter can behave like energy. Light can behave like waves or like particles. Atoms can behave like particles or like waves. In recognition of wave-particle duality (as it came to be called) physicists began using the term *matter wave* to describe both energy and atoms rather than specifying whether something is a particle or a wave.

The Uncertainty Principle

Soon after Dr. Jekyll and Mr. Hyde left physicists scratching their heads, another disconcerting discovery was made: We can't accurately measure all the properties of atomic-scale objects at the same time. Physicists found that a measurement of an atom could successfully reveal only one of two complementary properties with certainty; for example, you could know with certainty where an atom was (position), or you could learn where it was going and how fast it was going there (momentum). But you could never accurately know *both* position and momentum *at the same moment*. The more you know one, the less you know the other. This dilemma is referred to as the *Heisenberg uncertainty principle*.

The Intelligent-Observer Paradox

Compounding the discovery of nature's wave-particle duality and Heisenberg's uncertainty principle was the *intelligent-observer paradox*: the (still) astonishing fact that a matter wave takes on the behavior of matter only when it is measured by an intelligent observer. As we explored in Chapter 1, this mystifies most physicists, as well as most of the rest of us, to this day.

The best-known interpretation of these three counterintuitive discoveries is the Copenhagen interpretation, named after the home city of Neils Bohr, the father of quantum physics and the interpretation's primary exponent. The Copenhagen interpretation runs something like this: Get used to it. This is just the way it is. There is no point in asking why. Intelligent observers are needed in the formation of matter. Just accept that reality is weird. The only things we can know are the end results of observations and the accuracy of the math. There's nothing behind the curtain. There is no deeper reality. Reality is fundamentally weird, indeterminate, and random.

> Do not keep saying to yourself, if you can possibly avoid it, "But how can it be like that?" because you will get "down the drain," into a blind alley from which nobody has yet escaped. Nobody knows how it can be like that.
> —Richard Feynman, Nobel Prize–winning physicist[6]

I think of the Copenhagen and similarly oriented interpretations as the *pragmatic* interpretations. You can sum them up by the popular physics catch phrase, "Shut up and calculate." Such pragmatic interpretations allow scientists to acknowledge that there are weird aspects of reality, like the need for an intelligent observer, but at the same time allow them to minimize their importance. Instead of explaining the weird aspects of reality, they lump together the need for an intelligent observer with *non-locality* and *entanglement* (more on those coming up), call them all quantum weirdness, and simply ignore them.

The Copenhagen interpretation is an affirmation of scientific materialism's belief that everything that exists, and ever will exist, is the result of random matter-energy interactions, that reality is the accidental product of indeterminate forces. The Copenhagen interpretation leaves no room for the heavens, or anything like them, to have a guiding role in the formation of the universe.

Even while the Copenhagen interpretation gained acceptance in the 1920s and 1930s, many eminent scientists searched for a deeper order than the Copenhagen interpretation's pragmatism allowed. Einstein famously spoke against the random indeterminism of the Copenhagen interpretation. In a 1926 letter to Nobel Prize–winning physicist Max Born (1882–1970), he wrote:

> Quantum mechanics is certainly imposing. But an inner voice tells me that it is not yet the real thing. The theory says a lot, but does not really bring us any closer to the secret of the "old one." I, at any rate, am convinced that *He* does not throw dice.[7]

Einstein was convinced that the Copenhagen interpretation was flawed—an incomplete interpretation that told only part of the story. He was a proponent of alternative approaches, including what have come to be known as *hidden-variables* approaches, what we can also think of as *hidden-properties* approaches. According to the Copenhagen interpretation, the matter wave, while in the wave state, has no fixed properties. It takes on fixed properties only when measured by an intelligent observer. Before measurement, the matter wave is completely indeterminate—neutral energy able to take on any form.

Einstein felt that the matter wave only *appeared* to be indeterminate because, even though we cannot know all the properties of an atom at the same moment in time, these properties must nonetheless exist: They are simply *hidden* from us by the limitations of our understanding. He believed that the properties of all objects are, in fact, fixed or determinate, whether in the wave state or in the matter state. Einstein was convinced that Heisenberg's uncertainty principle and the measurement problem don't really exist but are simply mathematical phantoms of our incomplete knowledge.

Unfortunately for Einstein, during his lifetime his expectation of a hidden-properties solution not only did not emerge but in fact appeared to be completely ruled out by several mathematical proofs. These proofs prompted Bohr, the champion of the Copenhagen interpretation, to observe wryly that Einstein should stop telling God what to do with His dice. These mathematical proofs against hidden properties gave the upper hand to the Copenhagen interpretation's theory of fundamental indeterminate randomness.

Despite this setback, still convinced that God does not play dice, Einstein was not ready to give up on his belief in a determinate and ordered universe. He tried a different approach. He set out to show that quantum mechanics, along with its apparently mathematically proven indeterminate randomness, *had* to be flawed or incomplete because it led to *impossible* conclusions.

Using quantum physics' own equations, in 1935 Einstein and his colleagues, Podolsky and Rosen, wrote a paper showing that one could come to the mathematically inescapable conclusion that two particles could be *entangled* and could instantaneously "communicate" with each other over vast distances—*faster than the speed of light.* "Impossible!" cried Einstein. Relativity theory insists that nothing can go faster than the speed of light—not even something as formless as information. "Take that, quantum mechanics!" (politely) crowed Einstein.

Einstein's satisfaction with the findings of his paper was short lived. Although Einstein was confident that the impossibility of breaking the speed of light would show that the equations of quantum mechanics were significantly flawed, quantum physicists went on to prove that entangled particles *can* communicate information at speeds faster than light. Einstein had to go from crowing to eating crow.

To prove entanglement, physicists figured out how to split one high-energy photon into two lower-energy photon "twins." Once such twins are made, they remain permanently entangled; in the language of quantum physics they share one *quantum state*. Unlike identical twins, entangled twins always have *opposite* properties. If, for example, one photon twin has *right* polarization the other photon twin will always have *left* polarization.

If you recall, according to the Copenhagen interpretation all objects remain in an indeterminate wave state until they are measured by an intelligent observer. The logic of the Copenhagen interpretation is that until one twin is measured, both twins *could* have either right polarization or left polarization. But once one twin is measured by an intelligent observer, when the other twin is subsequently measured it will *always* have the opposite property. The second twin always "knows" the property the first twin "takes on" when measured—no matter how far apart the twins are when measured. Even if the twins were across the universe from each other, when one was measured the other would instantly take on the opposite properties—apparently communicating information at a speed vastly greater than the speed of light.

You can turn the *Twilight Zone* music back on.

Recent experiments have definitively confirmed this counterintuitive effect of entanglement. Physicists measured entangled particles many miles apart in a time interval of less than one part in 10,000 of the travel time of light between them.[8] Information would have to have traveled from one twin to the other at a minimum of 10,000 times the speed of light. The equations of quantum theory suggest, in fact, that the information is actually exchanged between the twinned photons *instantaneously*—and that it is only the limitations of our measuring devices that make it appear as if any time at all is required, however infinitesimal, for the entangled twins to communicate.[9]

Experimental verifications of entanglement appeared to rule out Einstein's hope for an ordered universe, one in which God did not play dice. Yet, ironically, it was the very notion of entanglement that spurred on one physicist, David Bohm, to discover the hidden properties in the cosmos that Einstein had been sure must exist.

Ever since Einstein and his colleagues put forward the idea of quantum entanglement, physicists have been trying to resolve its apparent violation of light's speed limit. There were three possibilities. One: There are essential flaws with the experiments proving entanglement. But after many years and thousands of experiments, no essential flaws have been found. Two: Information *can* travel through the universe faster than the speed of light. If this were the case, physicists would have to say goodbye to the theory of relativity, whose very foundation is the speed of light. Three: The counterintuitive concept that the physical universe is interpenetrated by a *nonlocal* realm must be accepted.

Nonlocal is an awkward term physicists use to describe a realm in which distance does not exist. An object or an event is considered to be *local* if it is subject to the effects of distance. Magnetic fields, for example, lose their strength over distance. It takes time for light to travel from the sun to the earth. These are *local effects*. On the other hand, and counterintuitively, objects or events in a nonlocal realm are unaffected by distance. Because the world we perceive around us through the senses *always* involves distance, we find it hard to imagine such a realm.

At first nonlocality was regarded as an abstract but meaningless artifact of the mathematics of quantum mechanics. But in a 1964 paper, "on the Einstein Podolsky Rosen paradox," John Stewart Bell presented a theorem that proved that not only *could* nonlocality be a property of reality, but that, according to the mathematical foundations of quantum physics itself, it *must* be.[10] In other words, you can't have one without the other. If quantum physics is true—and it has been proven to be true in countless applications—then nonlocality is a real property of the cosmos.

Many physicists do not know what to do with nonlocality. On the one hand, through Bell's theorem and many successful validations of entanglement, nonlocality is now an accepted and nonnegotiable feature of quantum physics. Remove it and quantum physics falls apart. On the other hand, many scientists simply do not want to go where nonlocality leads. Oxford University's Dr. David Deutsch wrote in an article for the *British*

Journal for the Philosophy of Science, "Despite the unrivalled empirical success of quantum theory, the very suggestion that it may be literally true as a description of nature is still greeted with cynicism, incomprehension, and even anger."[11]

One reason for the acceptance of the Copenhagen interpretation is its pragmatic encouragement to ignore nonlocality and other incomprehensible aspects of quantum weirdness. Quantum mechanics is a hugely successful tool for accomplishing things in the "real world" and, if this is one's goal, then for all practical purposes, nonlocality doesn't matter. You don't need to debate questions of randomness versus order, locality versus nonlocality—just shut up and calculate!

But not everyone is willing to shut up and calculate. David Bohm embraced rather than minimized the implications of quantum weirdness. By embracing *nonlocality*, especially, he was able mathematically to discover the order in the universe that had eluded Einstein. Bohm's work was groundbreaking. He developed a new mathematical system now called Bohmian Mechanics, and an interpretation of quantum physics bears his name.

David Bohm's long and fruitful career included being made a fellow of England's prestigious Royal Society, one of the highest accolades a scientist can receive, on par with receiving a Nobel Prize. Both a physicist and mathematician of note, Bohm, as a young doctoral candidate at UC Berkeley's department of physics, made a significant contribution to the Manhattan Project. Later, he made a number of discoveries in quantum and relativistic physics, including what has become known as *Bohm diffusion*. His book, *Quantum Theory*, published in 1951, remains a clear and concise explanation of basic quantum theory.

As his career progressed, however, Bohm grew dissatisfied with the Copenhagen interpretation's approach of ignoring quantum weirdness. Bohm instead embraced the fact of nonlocality, accepted its counterintuitive down-the-rabbit-hole implications, and set out to understand what it could mean. He came to the conclusion—startling but inescapable mathematically—that *the entire cosmos is one continuous interconnected whole.*

Appearances aside, he discovered mathematically that nothing can be separate from anything else, because the universe and everything in it is invisibly connected to a two-dimensional, nonlocal realm.

> [W]e say that inseparable quantum interconnectedness of the whole universe is the fundamental reality, and that relatively independent behaving parts are merely particular and contingent forms within this whole.
>
> —David Bohm[12]

> [The universe is] undivided wholeness in flowing movement.
>
> —David Bohm[13]

He called this nonlocal realm that connects everything *pre-space*. Pre-space, as the name implies, is *space-less*. In nonlocal pre-space, there is no distance as we understand the concept. According to Bohm, entangled photon twins, when measured by an intelligent observer, instantaneously enter our *space-full* three-dimensional world from this *space-less* pre-space. Bohm's work shows that were entangled photons instantaneously to appear in our physical universe billions of light years apart, the moment before their appearance they would have still been in space-less pre-space and thus, at the instant before their appearance, there would have been no distance between them at all. *what the fuck !!! ???*

Got it? I wouldn't be surprised if you don't, but hang in there. Understanding nonlocality is essential to understanding the physics of God.

Bohm's concept of nonlocal pre-space solves a number of nagging physics problems. It allows the speed of light in our local three-dimensional D-brane universe to remain unviolated while at the same time explaining the phenomenon of entanglement: Light always travels through three-dimensional space at a fixed and inviolate speed; but until the entangled twins *emerge* into three-dimensional space, with its fixed speed of light, they exist where there is no space and no distance, rendering the concept of speed meaningless.

Another nagging problem nonlocal pre-space solves is how matter knows how to form. If you recall, in Einstein's day mathematical proofs ruled out the possibility of hidden properties that would determine how matter formed, thus dashing Einstein's hope for the presence of hidden properties and apparently leaving us in a world where matter took a specific form only because of the chance presence of a specific intelligent observer. However, Bohm discovered, mathematically, that while hidden properties cannot exist in our *local* three-dimensional universe, as Einstein had hoped but math ruled out, hidden properties *can* exist in a *nonlocal*, two-dimensional pre-space without violating the mathematical proofs that ruled them out locally.

Got that? The Copenhagen interpretation tells us that the formation of matter is random and indeterminate and relies solely on the presence of an intelligent observer to determine its final form. Bohm's math, however, established that while form-determining hidden properties cannot exist in our *three-dimensional universe*, they could exist in *nonlocal two-dimensional pre-space*.

Bohm's work is highly significant. It offers a mathematically sound case that reality *is* determinate. Hidden properties, not random observations, determine the unfolding of the universe. Like many theories in physics, discoveries alternately appear to rule in and then rule out Bohm's approach. A 1992 paper apparently ruled out Bohmian Mechanics because it required a "surreal" motion for particles in double-slit experiments.[14] Now a 2016 paper apparently rules Bohmian Mechanics back in again, because the 1992 paper did not adequately account for nonlocality when considering the motion surreal.[15]

Bohm showed mathematically that the universe, and everything in it, emerges into physical being in conformance with a *hidden* order that exists in pre-space. He called this hidden order the *implicate order* and compared matter's process of emergence into physical being to that of something initially *folded* (flat, so to speak, in just two dimensions) then *unfolding* into three dimensions—*the explicate order*. The implicate part of the order exists in nonlocal pre-space. It serves as the template for (it provides the missing hidden properties for) the explicate order, which *unfolds* in our local three-dimensional universe according to the information in the enfolded order in pre-space, as Bohm describes here:

> In the enfolded [or implicate] order, space and time are no longer the dominant factors determining the relationships of dependence or independence of different elements. Rather, an entirely different sort of basic connection of elements is possible, from which our ordinary notions of space and time, along with those of separately existent material particles, are abstracted as forms derived from the deeper order. These ordinary notions in fact appear in what is called the "explicate" or "unfolded" order, which is a special and distinguished form contained within the general totality of all the implicate orders.[16]

Holograms

As his work progressed, Bohm also discovered that the mathematics governing how a hologram works provided an exceptionally useful mathematical model for how the implicate order, enfolded in nonlocal *two-dimensional* pre-space, allows the explicate order to unfold in local *three-dimensional* space. *Holograms* are two-dimensional. *Holographic projections* are three-dimensional. Holographic images are stored in *flat*, two-dimensional, media. When light interacts with the flat, two-dimensional media, however, a three-dimensional *holographic projection* appears. A holographic projection does not simply appear to be three-dimensional, it is: If one walks around a holographic projection one sees different sides of a three-dimensional object—all generated from two-dimensional media.

Bohm's work with the math behind holography has become known in physics as the *holographic principle*. It is not a fringe theory. Bohm's equations have become widely used in many branches of physics. After

Bohm's passing, the holographic principle became a major feature of string theory. Leonard Susskind, the Felix Bloch professor of theoretical physics at Stanford University and one of the fathers of string theory, fleshed out Bohm's holographic principle in the context of string theory. Gerard 't Hooft, a Dutch theoretical physicist at Utrecht University and co-winner of the Nobel Prize in physics in 1999, worked with Susskind to expand further on the holographic principle. In 1997, Juan Maldecena, professor of physics at Princeton's Institute of Advanced Studies, published a paper in which the holographic principle took center stage. By 2010, Maldecena's paper had been cited in papers by other physicists more than 7,000 times, and thus it became the most frequently cited paper in the field of high energy physics.[17]

The holographic principle, as it is used in string theory, states that the information determining the behavior of the three-dimensional volume of space we call the universe is "pasted on" the "boundary" between our three-dimensional universe and a two-dimensional brane. Put another way, the way the universe works—from the Big Bang to the present—is the result of information existing outside the universe itself. Put yet another way, light energy, interacting with a two-dimensional hologram in a two-dimensional brane, results in the colossal three-dimensional holographic projection we call the universe.

One's first encounter with the idea that the universe is a holographic projection can engender bemused disbelief or outright skepticism. The holographic projections with which we are familiar tend to be fuzzy and insubstantial, whereas the world we know is both finely detailed and solid. The fact that the world appears solid and finely detailed, however, does not negate the possibility that it is a holographic projection.

Most of you are aware that the images you see on your television or computer screen are made of dots. The dots are so tiny that you can only see them as dots if you use a magnifying glass. Taken together, these tiny dots form an image; the tinier the dots, the sharper the image. String theorists believe that the entire universe is made of dots inconceivably smaller than those on your screens—and not just in two dimensions as on your computer screen, but in three dimensions. Physicists tell us that the world we know appears solid and finely detailed because its "dots" are a *billion billion* times finer than the dots you see on a screen.

> Stanford physicist Leonard Susskind and Nobel Prize winner Gerard 't Hooft combine[d] quantum and relativistic descriptions of space-time. [M]athematically speaking, the fabric should be a 2D surface, and the grains should act like the dots in a vast cosmic image, defining the "resolution" of our 3D universe.
> —Victoria Jaggard, Smithsonian Online[18]

According to holographic string theory, if we could use an imaginary magnifying glass with unlimited magnification, we would be able to see that even *space* is made of dots. The physical universe, in the language of quantum physics, is *discontinuous*. It is not a seamless, continuous whole. We can fancifully imagine that what would "show through" between the dots, if we use our magnifying glass, is nonlocal, two-dimensional pre-space.

Einstein had the conviction that God does not play dice, that reality is ordered and determinate. He hoped to find the laws for such deterministic behavior within the *local* physical universe—but quantum mechanics ruled out the possibility. Bohm's deeper explorations of the weird side of quantum physics, and string theory's adoption of his holographic principle, strongly suggest that the order Einstein sought not only exists but is *nonlocal*. Ervin Laszlo, author of *Cosmos: A Co-creator's Guide to the Whole-World*, stated on the matter:

> We are beginning to see the entire universe as a holographically interlinked network of energy and information, organically whole and self-referential at all scales of its existence. We, and all things in the universe, are non-locally connected with each other and with all other things in ways that are unfettered by the hitherto known limitations of space and time.[19]

Bohm's mathematically sound interpretation of quantum physics, his implicate and explicate order, and string theory's use of his holographic principle all support the testimony of the saints, sages, and near-death experiencers: The heavens are the template for the universe. It doesn't take much of a leap to appreciate that Bohm's implicate order hidden in pre-space, or string theory's two-dimensional hologram hidden in a two-dimensional brane, could be dry scientific descriptions of a heavenly order hidden in what I call the *energy-verse*.

Science is a long way from being able to make such a leap. Scientific progress is ponderous and slow and requires exact proof every inch of the way. But the testimony of those who have witnessed the heavens directly is clear and consistent. I will take the liberty of repeating part of the quotations I used at the beginning of this chapter; in the light of what science has already revealed about the holographic principle these statements are even more telling—where there is a holographic projection there must be a hologram:

> In a word, absolutely everything in nature, from the smallest to the greatest, is a correspondence. The reason correspondences occur is that the natural world, including everything in it, arises and is sustained from the spiritual world.
> —Emanuel Swedenborg, Christian mystic[20]

Everything was created of spirit matter before it was created physically—solar systems, suns, moons, stars, planets, life upon the planets, mountains, rivers, seas, etc. This Earth is only a shadow of the beauty and glory of its spirit creation.
> —Betty J. Eadie, author of *Embraced by the Light*[21]

The blueprints of everything in the physical universe have been astrally conceived—all the forms and forces in nature, including the complex human body, have been first produced in that realm

where God's causal ideations are made visible in forms of heavenly light and vibratory energy.

—Paramhansa Yogananda, yoga master[22]

Perhaps the most significant implication of the holographic principle is that the universe is being *continuously created*. Most conceptions of
the creation of the universe—whether, for example, science's Big Bang or
Christianity's seven days of creation—suggest that, after an initial creative
event, physical creation remains as a permanent and independent reality.
The holographic principle suggests otherwise. It suggests that if the energy
that is interacting with the two-dimensional hologram in pre-space were
withdrawn, the three-dimensional holographic projection of the universe
would cease to exist—instantly. Furthermore, it suggests that the physical universe has no independent and enduring reality, that it is wholly
dependent, *moment by moment*, on the information and energy originating from the nonlocal, two-dimensional energy-verse.

You may be surprised to learn that saints and scientists alike concur
on this point:

God is creating the entire universe, fully and totally, in this present now. Everything God created . . . God creates now all at once.

—Meister Eckhart, Christian mystic[23]

The universe emerges out of an all-nourishing abyss not only
twelve billion years ago but in every moment.

—Brian Swimme, physicist[24]

My solemn proclamation is that a new universe is created every
moment.

—D.T. Suzuki, Zen teacher[25]

We are not stuff that abides, but patterns that perpetuate themselves; whirlpools of water in an ever-flowing river.

—Norbert Wiener, physicist[26]

The Tao is the sustaining Life-force and the mother of all things; from it, all things rise and fall without cease.

—Lao Tzu, *Tao Te Ching*

We have sought for firm ground and found none. The deeper we penetrate, the more restless becomes the universe; all is rushing about and vibrating in a wild dance.

—Max Born, Nobel Prize–winning physicist[27]

The energy-verse is an ocean of energy out of which our bubble-universe forms. The energy-verse contains the information, the hidden properties, the holographic template that makes our physical universe form as it does. Nor does creation take place once only; rather, the energy-verse continuously creates the physical universe. Without the holographic mechanism of creation, the universe would wink out of existence.

What scientists neutrally describe as an interpenetrating higher-frequency energy realm that creates the universe, the saints, sages, and near-death experiencers describe as an accessible, ordered, and entrancing realm of subtle energy. They tell us that this subtle realm, though invisible to our senses, is fully perceivable in transcendent states. Anyone who achieves perfect stillness and inner absorption, either through the practice of the science of religion or through the sudden stillness of death, will naturally and effortlessly perceive this subtler, ever-present reality that is hidden from our grosser physical senses and will see directly the heavenly holographic mechanism that creates the physical universe.

CHAPTER 6

Our Simultaneous Existence in Two Interpenetrating Realms

Not only do we exist in the three-dimensional physical universe, we also—simultaneously—exist in the two-dimensional energy-verse. The energy-verse continuously and invisibly interpenetrates the physical universe at every point.

> These heavenly realms, vibratory and transcendent, are only figuratively "above" the gross vibrations of earth "below": They are in fact superimposed one on the other.
>
> —Paramhansa Yogananda, yoga master[1]

Not only do we exist simultaneously in both realms, there is a continuous dynamic relationship between them that makes the physical universe inseparable from the energy-verse. What this means for us as individuals is that not only do we simultaneously inhabit both realms but also that our physical body is inseparable from our *energy body*:

- Like the universe, our physical body is *interpenetrated* at every point by the hidden-to-the-senses energies of the energy-verse.

103

- Like the universe, our physical body is an ultra-high definition *holographic projection*.
- Like the universe, our physical body is being *continuously created* according to the information in our own unique holographic energy template.

Saints, sages, and near-death experiencers tell us that we each have our own personal holographic energy template, or energy body. From this energy body the holographic projection of our physical body originates, and it determines, *moment by moment*, everything about our physical body. Our high-frequency energy body is variously called by the saints and sages the *astral body*, the *subtle body*, the *spirit body*, or sometimes, the *etheric body*. Our holographic energy body is made of coordinated energies vibrating at frequencies impossible for physical instruments to detect. Our physical body, on the other hand, is composed of detectable lower-frequency energy masquerading as matter; this lower-frequency energy is held in organized patterns by the interpenetrating higher-frequency energy body.

Despite not being able to perceive the interpenetrating subtle energy with our five senses, to one degree or another we are all aware of it. The experiential religious traditions of the world—from yoga to Sufism, to charismatic Christianity, to tai chi—call these subtle energies *life force*. An abundance of life force puts a bounce in our step and a smile on our face. It tingles through our body when we feel delight and knots our stomach when we're stressed. It warms our hearts when we feel love and tenses the body when we feel fear. It gives us an upward "rush" when we feel excited or inspired and drags us down when we are fatigued or depressed. It keeps the heart pumping, the lungs breathing, the digestion working, and it animates the myriad processes taking place in our trillions of cells. Without knowing precisely how we know, we are all aware of the presence of life force within us.

Working with life force is the heart of many alternative healing methods. There are many well-known and commonly accepted practices, such as the West's chiropractic and the East's acupuncture, which explain their success at improving health as the result of freeing blocked or impeded life force. Though sometimes still disparaged by the medical mainstream, these alternative methods are nonetheless so effective that many health insurance policies cover their use. It is hard to argue with results. Acupuncture has often been clinically tested and has been shown to be as effective, or more effective, than many conventional medical treatments for migraines,[2] lower back pain,[3] osteoarthritis,[4] and rheumatoid arthritis[5]—to name only a few.

Martial arts, in their highest expression, also work with a person's life force. Best known for amazing martial feats are the monks of the world famous Shaolin Temple in China: breaking bricks with the strike of a fist, breaking only one particular brick in a stack of bricks with the strike of a fist, using their chests to push with such force against the point of a sword that the sword is bent in two, having two spears pushed point first into their throats without wounding, or being held up in the air on the points of three or four spears without the skin being broken. Although it could be argued that a conventionally trained boxer could break boards and bricks as well as could a martial artist, it is hard to explain by conventional understanding how a person can be held aloft on the points of three or four spears—including one directly in the stomach—and not be impaled.

Further confirming the presence of life force, there are individuals, often called clairvoyants or intuitives, who can "see" the energy body. They perceive the energy body as a multicolored aura that surrounds and suffuses the physical body. Any change in a person's feelings, thoughts, and health is immediately apparent in the energy body: Colors move and change, colors become clearer or muddier, areas of the aura become brighter or dimmer, or the overall aura may expand or contract. Auras, also described as halos, are frequently depicted in religious paintings and sculptures. Every spiritual tradition describes saints and sages as being surrounded by a holy, otherworldly light.

I can tell you that anything that happens in the physical body will happen in the pattern of the energy fields first.

—Barbara Brennen, healer, author of *Hands of Light*[6]

Clairvoyants can see flashes of colour, constantly changing, in the aura that surrounds every person: each thought, each feeling, thus translating itself in the astral [energy] world, visible to the astral sight.

—Annie Besant, clairvoyant, Theosophical Society president[7]

At the heart of every experiential religious tradition in the world are techniques that enable one to become more aware of one's subtle energy body: meditation, tai chi, yoga postures, breathing techniques, and many more. In India's spiritual tradition, the life force is known as *prana*; in China, *chi* (also spelled *qi*). The ancient Egyptians referred to it as *ka*; the Greeks, *pneuma*. In Judaism, the life force is known as *ruach*; in Christianity, *spiritus*.

Learning to more deeply perceive and then control the subtle energy body is the first step on the journey to attaining the stillness and inner absorption that are essential to transcendent experience. Gaining greater awareness of subtle energy is universally recognized as the beginning of spiritual experience.

Those who become aware of their energy body—whether through subtle healing, martial arts, meditation, or intuitive perception—without exception reverently describe their experiences of their energy body as *sacred*. Experiencing one's life force more deeply is transformative. Attuning oneself to one's subtle energy body results in profound feelings of peace, harmony, expansion, calmness, well-being, joy, and an awed awareness of greater realities beyond the physical. In the Christian tradition, the life force is sometimes referred to as the *Holy Ghost* or *Holy Spirit*; in other traditions, the life force is considered to be the gateway to divine experience.

Do you not know that your bodies are temples of the Holy Spirit, who is in you, whom you have received from God?

—1 Cor. 6:19

Peace is the harmonious control of life. It is vibrant with life-energy. It is a power that easily transcends all our worldly knowledge. Yet it is not separate from our earthly existence. If we open the right avenues within, this peace can be felt here and now.

—Sri Chinmoy, Indian spiritual teacher[8]

I have come to understand from my personal experiences in meditation that my life-changing experience with hallucinatory drugs was in fact an unusually enhanced experience of my own life force—my sacred energy body. Today, by using techniques that increase my awareness of my energy body, such as meditation and *pranayama* (breathing techniques whose purpose is to make one more aware of prana or life force) I can experience that surpassing state of awareness—which I discovered accidentally through drugs—through much more reliable, consistent, and lasting means.

Where, you might be wondering, does the idea of life force and a subtle energy body coordinating and sustaining the physical body fit in with science and medicine? How far have string theory's vast conceptions of a multidimensional cosmos made their way into the human-sized life sciences such as biology and genetics? The short answer is: Not very far. Geneticists, neurobiologists, and medical researchers who have embraced the new multidimensional paradigm still get a chilly reception from the mainstream and have, so far, made little impact on the conventional biochemical model of the body.

The conventional biochemical model in medicine considers the body to be an amazing self-organizing and self-sustaining biochemical machine—but *only* a biochemical machine. According to this model, the body—composed of approximately 50 trillion cells—is maintained, not by an invisible interpenetrating energy-body, but by the brain and nervous system in close coordination with our genes.

This model maintains that all bodily processes—from voluntary movement to the continuous complex processes of circulation, digestion, assimilation, elimination, respiration, growth, and healing—are only *influenced* by electrochemical signals running through our nervous system and by biochemical messengers flowing through our circulatory system, but that the fundamental self-organizing life-processes are *orchestrated* by preprogrammed instructions coded into the DNA that makes up the genes found in the nucleus of our every cell. In the conventional model, the genes in the nucleus of the cell are that cell's *brain*, and collectively, the brains of 50 trillion cells work together remarkably seamlessly to keep us alive and healthy.

DNA (deoxyribonucleic acid) is made up of two long chains of four nucleic acids in varying sequences—(G) guanine, (A) adenine, (T) thymine, and (C) cytosine—coiling around each other to form a double helix (Figure 8). Our DNA contains sequentially encoded "blueprints" for making complex proteins, which are the building blocks and catalysts for growing, healing, and sustaining our bodies. Varied sequences of the

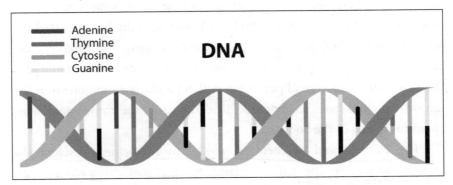

FIGURE 8. *The basic structure of DNA: two long chains of nucleic acids that coil around each other, forming a double helix as a result of the attraction of pairs of nucleic acids—adenine to thymine and cytosine to guanine.*

four nucleic acids, G, A, T, and C—somewhat analogous to the 1s and 0s of binary computer code—contain, it is widely believed, the information necessary to build, and to know when to build, all the proteins necessary to maintain the structure and functions of our bodies.

Our cells are, to a large extent, protein factories. To produce a protein, first the DNA in the nucleus relaxes its tightly coiled double helix shape along a short segment of its full length (rather like twisting open and stretching out just a few coils in a long spring), thereby exposing a segment of the DNA strand that contains the coded blueprint for one particular protein. Once the DNA uncoils, another type of molecule (very similar to DNA, called messenger RNA or mRNA) begins to form, amino acid by amino acid, along one strand of the exposed DNA (Figure 9). The result is a new chain of amino acids that *exactly* matches the sequence of the DNA chain. Now a perfect copy of the sequence exposed by the DNA and a blueprint for a single protein, the mRNA "unzips" from the DNA and exits the nucleus.

Once it leaves the nucleus, the RNA is grabbed by a ribosome. Ribosomes, which are protein-making machines in the cell, connect together one amino acid after another in a long chain exactly matching the sequence coded in the RNA (Figure 10). As the chain lengthens, it folds upon itself, creating a distinct size and shape. Proteins can be made from hundreds or even thousands of amino acids connected together in an exact sequence. The protein, once created, is put to work in the cell's structure, or in the cell's processes (such as binding or catalyzing), or it is sent out of the cell to where it is needed for other life processes such as digestion or hormonal regulation.

Our cells are incredibly prolific protein factories. It takes only seconds for each ribosome to produce a finished protein molecule containing as many as several thousand amino acids. Each of our body's cells can produce hundreds of thousands, even millions, of protein molecules in a single day; and each cell is theoretically capable of producing every one of the 20 million different proteins encoded in human DNA.

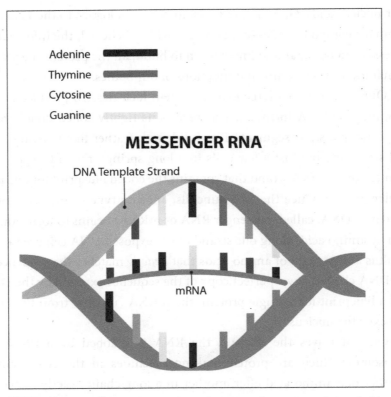

FIGURE 9. *Messenger RNA forms along the exposed sequence of uncoiled DNA.*

Most microbiologists and geneticists share the opinion that not only are all the blueprints for all the proteins the body needs contained in our DNA, but that all the information an organism needs to grow and maintain itself (that is, all the information that determines *when and in what combinations to build specific proteins*) is also contained in our DNA. According to this belief, the DNA in every cell is hard coded like a computer to regulate what and when proteins are needed: From the beginning of life in the womb to the passing from life in death, every infinitesimally small biochemical interaction is predetermined by and preprogrammed in our DNA.

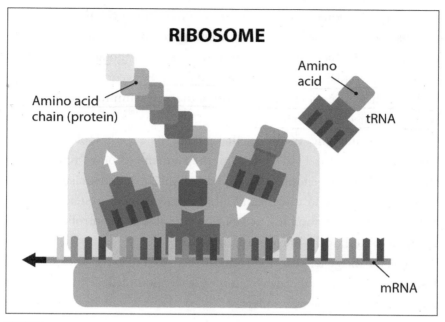

FIGURE 10. *Messenger RNA moves through a ribosome, a protein-building machine, and the encoded sequence in the mRNA determines the order in which amino acids are added to a long chain which folds on itself, forming a protein.*

We are, from the point of view of the conventional model, nothing more than amazingly complex biochemical machines that have slowly evolved over billions of years from the accidental combinations of chemicals—the primordial soup—and serendipitous environmental events such as lightning strikes or contact with crystals. Intelligence is considered an accidental by-product of evolution; music, literature, human nobility, self-sacrifice, love—all are considered the random outgrowths of survival-increasing mutations.

In this model, everything is neatly explained by scientific materialism. No weird, holographic energy body template required, thank you very much. Life force? Who needs it?

The conventional biochemical story of life, with DNA in the starring role, has held sway for decades. But, contrary to popular opinion, the biochemical model has never been fully elucidated. Although most geneticists *believe* that DNA is preprogrammed for every eventuality from birth to death, they have yet to *identify* most of the programming that would be needed for their belief to be true.

You can imagine, therefore, that geneticists eagerly looked forward to the revelations surely to come from the Human Genome Project. Once the entire human genome was sequenced in 2003, geneticists thought they would be able to understand all the unexplained mysteries of how the encoded information in our DNA coordinates and controls the life of every cell and thus the life of every organism.

Alas for the geneticists, the Human Genome Project did not solve the last mysteries. In fact, those mysteries were compounded. Denise Chow, in an article for LiveScience, explained:

> When the human genome was sequenced, some scientists were saying, "That's the end. We're going to understand every disease. We're going to understand every behavior." And it turns out, we didn't, because the sequence of the DNA isn't enough to explain behavior. It isn't enough to explain diseases.[9]

In a commentary on the surprising results of the Human Genome Project, David Baltimore, one of the world's preeminent geneticists and a Nobel Prize winner, addressed the issue of human complexity: "But unless the human genome contains a lot of genes that are opaque to our computers, it is clear that we do not gain our undoubted complexity over worms and plants by using more genes."[10]

Bruce Lipton continued the discussion with his own thoughts in *The Biology of Belief*: "Understanding what does give us our complexity— our enormous behavioral repertoire, ability to produce conscious action, remarkable physical coordination, precisely tuned alterations in response to external variations of the environments, learning, memory, need I go on?—remains a challenge for the future.[11]

Not finding the preprogramming for all of life encoded in our genes has forced geneticists into a fundamental reassessment of how our genes function. This reassessment has been strongly influenced by relatively recent discoveries that have led to the establishment of a new discipline in genetics known as *epigenetics*—literally, "above the gene." These discoveries indicate that our genes are not fixed—that what were previously considered permanently dormant genes can become active and active genes can become deactivated. These discoveries cast significant doubt on the long-held belief that DNA is the brain of the cell. It looks more and more likely that our cells are controlled from another source.

Epigenetics was born when geneticists were astonished to learn that *newly awakened* genetic traits *can be passed down from one generation to the next*. Scientists in Sweden conducted transgenerational research on people living in the Overkalix area in northern Sweden. They discovered that parents who had experienced famine conditions passed on famine-compensating physiological traits to their children. Prior to this 1995 study, altering genetic traits and then passing the altered traits on to progeny was considered impossible. This study turned the bedrock belief that gene expression was fixed and immutable upside down.[12]

Another one of the outcomes of the complete sequencing of the human genome was the discovery that there aren't enough protein-producing genes to produce all 20 million proteins that we know the human body produces. During the sequencing of the human genome, it was shown that we have only 20,000 to 25,000 protein-producing genes—not nearly enough if each protein-producing gene were able only to produce one protein. This led to the understanding that the actual *gene expression* of one particular gene can vary enormously. We now know that every *protein-producing gene is able to produce many different proteins.*

For some time now it has been thought that only roughly 1.5 to 2 percent of the genes in our DNA are active; the rest are permanently dormant. In the conventional model, the remaining inactive genes are believed to be the remnants of a long evolutionary process and no longer useful to us in our current evolutionary state. Recent studies have shown, however, that we activate and inactivate our own genes routinely—not just in rare cases like the Overkalix study identified.

Throughout the course of three months, a group of more than 30 men with low-risk prostate cancer, following an intensive nutrition and lifestyle regimen, upregulated 48 genes that help the body fight tumors and downregulated 453 genes that tend to promote tumors.[13] More amazing yet are the number of epigenetic changes made over a six-month period in a Swedish study of 23 slightly overweight men attending spinning and aerobics classes twice per week. Researchers at Lund University discovered that the men had epigenetically altered 7,000 genes—almost 30 percent of all the genes in the entire human genome![14]

From these and other studies, we now know that *environmental, behavioral, mental, and emotional changes* can turn on thousands of genes once considered permanently dormant, or turn off genes once considered to be permanently active.

The new paradigm that is emerging from these various genetic and epigenetic studies is that one set of genetic blueprints can produce many different results. Twins who begin their lives with identical portions of their DNA activated can end their lives with very different portions of their DNA activated. There is no inevitable, preprogrammed, hard-coded destiny in our genes; outside influences, such as behaviors, and even our thoughts and feelings can substantially alter gene activation and gene expression.

It is impossible to reconcile the new evidence of flexible gene expression with the idea that DNA is the preprogrammed brain of the cell. Our DNA turning on and turning off genes by itself would be rather like Escher's famous *Drawing Hands*, in which one hand is drawing another hand while the other hand is drawing the first hand, or a computer that can independently decide what programs to run.

How, then, *can* an outside influence turn genes on and off or alter the gene expression of the same gene—something that according to the conventional model is impossible? The key may be found in the emerging field of *quantum biology.*

Quantum biology, as the name implies, is the study of quantum effects, specifically nonlocal quantum effects, in living systems. Until recently, nonlocal quantum effects were believed to be impossible in the warm, moist environment of living systems. However, fascinating new discoveries have shown that belief was mistaken.

The first and most well-established discovery of quantum biology is its explanation for the amazing efficiency of photosynthesis.[15] Scientists have long known that photosynthesis in plants is far more efficient at capturing the energy of the sun than any nonliving chemical processes can duplicate. It turns out that the reason for photosynthesis's amazing efficiency is *quantum entanglement.*

The chlorophyll molecule's job is to transfer the sun's energy to a photoreaction center where the sun's electromagnetic energy is converted to chemical energy. Quantum biologists have recently discovered that hundreds, even thousands, of chlorophyll molecules, when transferring the sun's energy, vibrate in *perfect synchronization with one another.* They do so by forming a liquid crystal—that is, they align in exactly the same way, in exactly the same phase (like rowers stroking in perfect rhythm), and in exactly the same frequency. This perfectly coordinated synchrony turns all the chlorophyll molecules into a kind of biological superconductor, thereby enabling the super-efficient transfer of sunlight quanta from one chlorophyll molecule to the next. The phenomenon is called *resonant energy transfer.*

This may sound like just another wonder of science, but such coordinated molecular resonance does not occur in nonliving systems. In fact, according to conventional thinking in quantum mechanics, every chlorophyll molecule should be dancing to its own tune—out of alignment, out of frequency, and out of phase with all the other chlorophyll molecules. In the language of quantum physics, every chlorophyll molecule should behave *decoherently*.

Instead, the chlorophyll molecules are behaving coherently. To have hundreds, or even thousands, of chlorophyll molecules in the same alignment, phase, and frequency means that all of these molecules must be sharing the same quantum state; put another way, the hundreds or thousands of chlorophyll molecules must be *quantumly entangled*.

In the last chapter we explored the idea of entanglement. I described experiments in which photon twins share a single quantum state. Resonant energy transfer in living plants works similarly but on a scale far beyond twinned photons. Hundreds to thousands of chlorophyll molecules are held *indefinitely* in a single quantum state.

In the last chapter we also explored the idea that the energy realm contains the holographic template for the physical realm and thus contains the information that determines all physical properties and behavior. If thousands of chlorophyll molecules are being held in an entangled coherent state, then the *information*—the determining cause of the coherent state—is coming from the nonlocal energy-verse, not from the local physical universe. Put simply, the plant's holographic energy template is *controlling* the chlorophyll molecules by holding them in a shared quantum state.

The discovery of resonant energy transfer in plants is part of a wave of discoveries of other nonlocal quantum effects in other living organisms. Evidence suggests that the tissues of all living organisms are frequently found in coherent entangled states. One key piece of evidence is the discovery of the ubiquitous presence of *liquid crystals* in the tissues of all living organisms.

The atoms or molecules of *solid* crystals, from ice to salt to diamonds, align in a uniform lattice structure. The lattice structure gives crystals qualities that ordinary solids made of the same atoms or molecules do not have. The classic example is coal and diamond. Carbon, in a non-crystal form such as coal, is relatively soft and opaque; carbon in a crystalline form such as diamond is extremely hard and translucent. A crystal's ordered structure imparts to it many properties, such as enhanced electrical conductivity, that ordinary solids made of the same atoms or molecules do not have.

Liquid crystals share many of the properties of solid crystals but, as the name implies, a liquid crystal has the flexibility of a liquid while its molecules nonetheless can remain oriented in a lattice. Like solid crystals, liquid crystals have properties that amorphous collections of the same molecules do not have.

Biologists are now finding organic liquid crystal structures throughout living organisms. In a 1998 study, "Organisms as Polyphasic Liquid Crystals," geneticist and quantum biologist Mae-Wan Ho and her team pioneered a novel interference color-imaging technique, which enabled her team to detect, non-invasively, liquid crystalline domains in living organisms.[16] They were amazed to find them virtually everywhere in living tissues. What's more, Ho's team discovered that organic liquid crystals, unlike solid crystals, can be more and less in phase, that is, the liquid crystal's alignment, phase, and frequency can become more or less pronounced: Thus, they are polyphasic.

Other studies have revealed that the cell walls of all 50 trillion cells in an adult human body behave as liquid crystals. The molecules that form the cell wall are said to have the shape of lollipops: The head of the lollipop is oriented outward to form a barrier and the handle of the lollipop is pointing inside toward the center of the cell. This coordinated *crystalline alignment* of the lollipops creates an impermeable barrier to atoms and molecules outside the cell. There is also an inner cell wall that forms in the same way, except that the heads of the lollipops are oriented toward the inside of the cell and the handles toward the outer wall, thus forming a perfect inner barrier just inside the outer barrier.

The liquid crystalline cell wall controls independently one of the most important functions of the cell. By changing the crystalline lattice orientation of the lollipop-shaped molecules to create openings, the cell wall lets in only what it wants to let in and lets out only what it wants to let out. In *The Biology of Belief*, Bruce Lipton explains:

> Cell biologists gained insight into the amazing abilities of the cell membrane by studying the most primitive organisms on this planet, the prokaryotes. Prokaryotes, which include bacteria and other microbes, consist only of a cell membrane that envelops a droplet of soupy cytoplasm. Though prokaryotes represent life in its most primitive form, they have purpose. A bacterium does not bounce around in its world like a ball in a pinball machine. A bacterium carries out the basic physiologic processes of life like more complicated cells. A bacterium eats, digests, breathes, excretes waste matter, and even exhibits "neurological" processing. They can sense where there is food and propel themselves to that spot. Similarly, they can recognize toxins and predators and purposely employ escape maneuvers to save their lives. In other words, prokaryotes display intelligence! So what structure in the prokaryotic cell provides its "intelligence"? The prokaryotes' cytoplasm has no evident organelles, such as the nucleus and mitochondria, which are found in more advanced, eukaryotic cells. The only organized cellular structure that can be considered a candidate for the prokaryote's brain is its cell membrane.[17]

Another confirmation of the ubiquitous presence of liquid crystals in the body is based on the 1920s discovery by the Russian embryologist Alexander Gurwitch. He discovered that our bodies emit very weak photons, called biophotons. His discovery has long been known and is widely accepted. In the 1970s, Fritz-Albert Popp and researchers at the University of Marburg in Germany, later at the Institute of Biophysical Cell Research in Germany, applied Gurwitch's discovery to exploring the crystalline structure of the human body.

What Popp's team expected to find, based on the conventional biochemical model, is that *every* biophoton emission would be emitted at random times and at random frequencies. Instead, they found that almost *all* biophoton emissions were emitted in phase—same timing, same frequency. Their findings suggest that, just as chlorophyll molecules are aligned and synchronized during resonant energy transfer, *most tissues in the human body are in continuously entangled, coherent quantum states.*

A recent paper on the behavior of brain cells, published in the journal *Neuron*, reveals that brain cells often change their rate of vibration, referred to in the paper as "theta and low- and high-frequency gamma oscillations."[18] Further, the study authors found that separate groups of brain cells, located in different regions of the brain, will often be in the same frequency and phase. •

Significantly, it has also been discovered that DNA, too, behaves as a liquid crystal.[19]

If, contrary to the conventional biochemical model and conventional genetic theory, DNA is only a *collection of blueprints* for creating proteins—but does not itself contain preprogrammed coding to control the timing and use of the protein blueprints—then the controlling information that determines what proteins are produced, and when, has to come from somewhere else. Quantum biology suggests that the controlling information is nonlocal; string theory's holographic principle suggests that the controlling information is contained in a nonlocal holographic energy template: Through the nonlocal-to-local information bridge, known as quantum entanglement or quantum coherence, a holographic energy template can control the liquid crystal DNA molecule and coordinate what proteins a cell makes and when.

Informed by the discoveries of epigenetics and quantum biology explored previously, a new quantum biological model is emerging. Although known biochemical processes are unquestionably taking place continuously in living organisms, there is another, subtler process taking place as well: The liquid crystal structures within our tissues, including DNA, phase in and out of quantum coherence—thus allowing the information from our holographic energy template to initiate and coordinate the life processes taking place in our physical body.

> It is the failure to transcend the [biochemical] mechanistic framework that makes people persist in enquiring which parts [of the body] are in control, or issuing instructions or information. The challenge for us all is to rethink information processing in the context of the [quantumly] coherent organic whole.
>
> —Mae-Wan Ho, geneticist and quantum biologist[20]

> A subtle spiritual mechanism is hidden just behind the bodily structure.
>
> —Sri Yukteswar[21]

> We must liberate man from the cosmos created by the genius of physicists and astronomers, that cosmos in which, since the renaissance, he has been imprisoned. We now know that we . . . extend outside the physical continuum. . . . In time, as well as in space, the individual stretches out beyond the frontiers of his body. . . . He also belongs to another world.
>
> —Dr. Alexis Carrel, Nobel Prize winner[22]

This new quantum-biologic paradigm, in which liquid crystal domains in our physical body phase in and out of coherent quantum entanglement with a nonlocal template-like energy body, explains many things that the conventional model cannot.

In the conventional model, it is very difficult to account for the astonishing degree of coordination of all the biochemical processes taking place in the human body. There are approximately 50,000 biochemical events taking place in each and every cell, *each and every second*. If we multiply the 50,000 biochemical events in each cell by 50 trillion—a medium estimate of the number of cells in an adult human body—then we find there are *50 quadrillion coordinated biochemical events* taking place in the human body *every second.*

With the concept of DNA as the preprogrammed brain of the cell no longer likely, then according to the conventional biomechanical model, *all* the coordination of this astonishing complexity would have to fall to the brain and nervous system. Yet as complex as the brain and nervous system is, it is neither fast enough nor vast enough to exert control over quadrillions of events per second.

As an example, the startling result of a study conducted by C.F. Hebb proves that, according to the biochemical model of the body, it would be *impossible* for a pianist to play a rapid piece of music! After careful study, he concluded that the turnaround time for neuronal signals to be sent to the brain from the hands, for them to be integrated in the brain, and then for new neuronal signals to be sent back to the hands is simply too long for the pianist to be able to coordinate his hands while playing advanced pieces. In a piece played *prestissimo* (the fastest of musical tempos at 200 or more beats per minute), a pianist has to be able to play multiple notes before the roundtrip to the brain and back can be completed.[24]

How, then, could the nervous system control 50 quadrillion biochemical events per second if it can't control a pianist's rapid fingering? If instead the coordination were conducted through our body's tissues while in entangled coherent states, the signals would move instantaneously through the essentially distance-less, nonlocal energy realm that interpenetrates our body.

There is another major problem with the conventional non-quantum biochemical model: It cannot explain rapid, even instantaneous, physiological changes in the human body. Of all the supporting arguments for the presence of an entangled holographic energy body, instantaneous physiological change is perhaps the most compelling. And the most compelling source of evidence of instantaneous physiological change, as mentioned in Chapter 1, is the studies of those with multiple-personality disorder (MPD). MPD sufferers have often been observed, in controlled clinical conditions, to manifest astonishingly rapid physiological changes.

Multiple-personality disorder (MPD) causes the sufferer to express many different personalities. Each personality is distinct. Each personality has particular characteristics and tendencies. Each personality has a unique set of memories. Some personalities are young children even when the MPD sufferer is an adult. Different personalities often respond to different names. Some have talents, such as being able to play a musical instrument that the other personalities cannot play. Some personalities can even speak foreign languages that the others cannot.

Less well known is that each personality undergoes distinct physiological changes—some quite dramatic—when transitioning (in a time period ranging from seconds to minutes) from one personality to the next. Dr. Philip M. Coons, who compiled the results of more than 50 studies regarding physiological changes among MPD sufferers, documents that the rapid physiological changes of MPD sufferers have been measured using modern medical devices and techniques including electroencephology, visual evoked responses, galvanic skin responses, electromyography, regional cerebral-blood-flow monitoring, voice spectral analysis, brain electrical activity mapping, and electrocardiography.[24] Measurements taken using these instruments as well as systematic observational methods leave no doubt that physiological changes do emerge and then vanish when one personality changes to another. In other words, what you are about to read is not in doubt. It is well-documented and was measured using sophisticated scientific instruments.

Voice spectral-analysis reveals one's unique voice fingerprint or *voiceprint*. Even exceptional mimics, who can sound convincingly like many well-known people, cannot fool voice spectral-analysis—their underlying voiceprint remains unchanged regardless of the imitation they are performing, just as an actor playing many parts always has the same fingerprints. On the other hand—and impossibly, according to the conventional biochemical model—MPD personalities often have a unique voiceprint for each personality.

According to the conventional biochemical model, our genes determine the physical structures that give rise to our unique voiceprint. According to the logic of the conventional biochemical model, for each MPD personality to have its own unique voiceprint, each MPD personality would have to be manifesting a unique gene expression—perhaps even unique genes. MPD personalities have been observed to write with different hands, that is, the left or the right. Handedness is conventionally considered to be genetically determined. What the observed facts indicate is that MPD sufferers manifest physiological changes that can only be explained as arising from *instantaneous genetic changes*.

One personality can suffer from allergies, such as to bee stings, while the individual's other personalities do not. One personality can be diabetic, a condition that takes years to develop and insulin to manage, while the others are not. As mentioned in Chapter 1, each MPD personality can have different visual characteristics. MPD sufferers have been measured carefully by ophthalmologists for refraction (by measuring refraction errors or astigmatisms), visual acuity (by measuring focal ability, for example, 20/20 vison), ocular tension (by measuring the intraocular pressure), keratometry (by measuring the curve of the cornea), and color vision (by measuring how accurately colors are detected).

In one particular study, a MPD sufferer moved through 10 personalities in less than an hour. An ophthalmologist was on hand to do a complete set of measurements for each personality. Once the results were examined it was found that *the eyes of each of the 10 personalities had significantly different visual characteristics from the other nine*. These are not the normal physiological changes that anyone's eyes might go through over a period of time—however long. It is as though the eyes of each personality belong to an entirely different body. In other studies, some personalities are color-blind for blue and green while the others are not. One personality has an astigmatism while the others do not. One personality even has an iris colored differently from the irises of the others.

One MPD sufferer would manifest needle tracks on his arms only when a personality emerged that believed he was a drug addict—even though no drugs had been injected. Rashes, moles, scars, and other skin conditions emerge and vanish as personalities come and go. A personality of a young boy reacted to poison ivy, including having fluid-filled blisters on his skin. On switching to another personality, the blisters vanished in minutes.

The fascinating list of physiological anomalies found among MPD sufferers goes on and on. But all the strange and unusual clinically observed phenomena have one thing in common—*they are all impossible*—at least according to the conventional biochemical model of how our bodies work. The body-as-a-biological-machine concept provides no explanation for how any of these phenomena could have happened. According to the conventional model, none of these changes should have been able to take place with the rapidity they have; many of these changes, such as different voiceprints, handedness, eyesight, colorblindness, or iris color should not be able to occur successively in one body—period—because they would require the presence of different genes.

How, then, can such changes happen?

The visible world is the invisible organization of energy.
—Heinz Pagels, former executive director,
New York Academy of Sciences[25]

Our body, like the universe, is being *continuously created* from our template-like holographic energy body. The moment change occurs in our holographic energy body is the moment change occurs in the holographic projection we know as our physical body. Our physical bodies are not fixed—they are energy masquerading as matter. Nor do they exist independently. Our physical bodies are the moment-by-moment result of *nonlocal* energies interacting with our *nonlocal* two-dimensional holographic energy template, resulting in our *local*, holographically projected, three-dimensional physical body.

The conventional biochemical-machine model of the body has no answer for how instantaneous changes can occur. The quantum-biological paradigm, on the other hand, in which the physical body is inseparably entangled with an interpenetrating holographic energy body, *does* have an answer. Our physical body is the result of the invisible organization of energy; change the organization of the energy, no matter how fast, and you change the physical body just as fast.

The scientifically grounded idea that we exist simultaneously in multiple realms goes far beyond providing a new model for living systems; the idea that we exist simultaneously in multiple realms also opens the door for science to understand how there can be *life after death*. From the point of view of the conventional biochemical model—with its premise that biochemical life is purely physical—life after death is impossible. From the point of view of the multidimensional quantum-biological model, *we already exist in the afterlife*.

Physical death is the withdrawal of the invisible organization of energy from the physical body. When the influence of the template-like holographic energy-body is withdrawn, the physical body loses its coordinated entangled coherence with its holographic energy body. Coherence gone, the physical body begins to respond to the forces of entropy—order goes to disorder, energy dissipates to equilibrium—and the physical body decays into lifeless atoms and molecules.

Even when the physical body stops functioning, however, our energy-body continues to exist. Think of your physical body as a sock puppet. When the hand is withdrawn from the sock, the sock puppet "dies," but the hand that was inside the puppet continues to exist. Our nonlocal, interpenetrating energy-body is the hand within the sock puppet.

What the saints, sages, and near-death experiencers tell us is that when we die, we no longer perceive through the low-frequency detectors that we know as the physical senses; instead, we immediately begin perceiving our higher-frequency energy body and the energy-verse through subtler means.

> Using radio as an analogy, this speed-up is comparable to having lived all your life at a certain radio frequency when all of a sudden someone or something comes along and flips the dial. That flip shifts you to different frequency. The original frequency where you once existed is still there. It did not change. Everything is still just the same as it was. Only you changed, only you speeded up to allow entry into the next radio frequency on the dial. You fit your particular spot on the dial by your speed of vibration. You shift frequencies in dying. You switch over to life on another wavelength. You are still a spot on the dial but you move up or down a notch or two. You don't die when you die. You shift your consciousness and speed of vibration. That's all death is . . . a shift.
>
> —P.M.H. Atwater, near-death experiencer, NDE researcher, and author of *Beyond the Light*[26]

> There are many realms that take up the same space as the physical realm much like boxes within boxes. The physical realm is but one of the boxes in the hierarchy of boxes. This means we are actually already in the so-called afterlife right now.
>
> —Kevin Williams, near-death researcher and author of *Nothing Better than Death*[27]

> Never before had I considered that there might be such things as coexistent realities. Never had I imagined that there might be concurrent realms. I realized that in life, death is merely the other side of a threshold over which I could not "normally" see. So, too, in death, life and the land of the "living" were on the other side of a very thin veil.
>
> —Lynnclaire Dennis, author of *The Pattern*[28]

Our physical body is controlled, sustained, and created, moment by moment, by our energy body. Quantum entanglement of our energy body with our physical liquid-crystal tissues is the bridge that allows the holographic information contained in our energy-body to affect the physical body. Our DNA is only a set of blueprints. The choice of which protein blueprint to build is communicated not from predetermined coding of our DNA, but from our energy-body hologram to our physical body. Instantaneous physiological change is possible because the light-show illusion of our body is organized energy masquerading as matter. Change the organization, no matter how rapidly, and the physical body will change just as rapidly.

We already inhabit our energy-body. We feel and interact with our energy-body all the time—not just when we die. We feel it and experience it at every moment, even though we can't perceive it directly with our physical senses. Our energy body is the source of our life-energy, our feelings, our likes and dislikes, our motivations. *The energy-body is the source of most of what we think of as ourselves.* It is constantly, dynamically, and integrally *us*.

Death is only the loss of our *physical* body, the shedding of a suit of clothes that covers the energy-body; it is not the end of our existence. Once the physical body dies, we adjust to being aware of our energy-body only. And once we are beyond the confining limitations of our physical body—as the saints, sages, and near-death experiencers all testify—we will experience a freedom and awareness unlike anything that can be experienced through the physical body.

CHAPTER 7

The Intelligently Guided Cosmic Movie

String theory's holographic principle suggests that the physical universe is a cosmic movie: The three-dimensional holographic projection we call the universe is created by the universe's nonlocal two-dimensional holographic energy template interacting with the energy-verse's higher frequency energies, like light being shown through film in a projector.

But how does the holographic "film" get made? Why does the two-dimensional energy-verse, which contains the heavens and the template for the entire universe, have the high degree of intelligent order that it does?

We've already encountered some clues to help answer that question: the MPD sufferers' ability to change their physical bodies; the placebo effect; PEAR's proof that individuals can affect the outcomes of physical processes; the CIA's Stargate's proof that information can be shared from mind to mind; and quantum physics' double-slit experiments indicating that an intelligent observer must be present for energy to change from its wave state to its particle state.

The common element in all these clues is *intelligent consciousness*. From nonlocal intelligent consciousness comes the information—and the inherent laws—that creates the holographic "film" that, in turn, creates the cosmic movie we know as the universe. Our own intelligent consciousness creates our own hologram that, in turn, creates our own small part of the cosmic movie we think of as our physical body.

Most of us take our own intelligence and consciousness for granted. Most of us experience our thoughts as passing ephemera without a noticeable connection to our physical body or the world around us. But, as you may be appreciating more and more, your thoughts are *powerful*; they are, for example, continuously, moment-by-moment, determining your appearance and physical health.

In our everyday experience, we don't see our appearance and physical health fluctuating and changing with our every conscious thought because the thoughts that determine our appearance and physical health are deep, subconscious, unquestioningly held convictions that, even when we want to, are difficult to change. Our slow-to-change, deeply held thoughts are therefore equally slow to change our physical body. If we developed the ability immediately to change our deeply held thoughts, however, we could immediately change our physical bodies at will.

MPD sufferers' bodies change all but instantaneously. As each personality emerges with its unquestioningly held, deeper-than-conscious convictions about that personality's appearance, state of health, and physical abilities, each personality's body immediately changes to conform to those convictions. Once MPD sufferers shift into new personalities, each personality has the *absolute* conviction that *its* body will be as it expects that body to be—the drug-user personality expecting to see needle tracks on his arms, or the woman expecting to see green eyes looking back at her in the mirror, even though all the other personalities that share that body have brown eyes.

Most of us, fortunately, do not suffer from multiple-personality disorder, but our thoughts are just as powerful, even though we might not witness that power so instantaneously. In 1968, researchers Luparello and Bleeker conducted a medical trial for asthma inhalers. Forty actual asthma sufferers were given inhalers, which they were told contained an irritant. In fact, the inhalers contained nothing but water vapor. Nonetheless, after using the inhaler, almost half of the test group experienced such asthmatic symptoms as restriction of their airways, and about 30 percent suffered full asthmatic attacks. The researchers then gave each asthma sufferer a new inhaler, which they were told contained a medicine that could relieve their symptoms. These inhalers, too, contained nothing but water vapor. Nonetheless, every asthma sufferer recovered.[1]

As mentioned in Chapter 1, a 1976 drug trial for a potential chemo-therapy treatment for gastric cancer was conducted by the British stomach-cancer group. The results of the study were published in the May 1983 *World Journal of Surgery*.[2] Four hundred and eleven patients participated. During the course of the study, which lasted several months, 30 percent of the patients given only a placebo saline drip with no active ingredients *lost all their hair.*

The placebo testing method has been used even for surgical proce-dures.[3] The placebo patients are given a sham surgery—rolled in to the operating room, given anesthesia, incised, sutured back together, and then given post-operative care—all with no actual procedural surgery having been performed. In these cases also, a high percentage of the trial patients who have had the sham surgery become cured of significant preexisting physical problems.

As these examples show, people who have received placebos or pla-cebo treatments—yet believed they were getting a trial drug or a new sur-gical procedure—manifest significant physiological changes. Nor is it only a small percentage of the placebo group who respond. Placebo takers con-sistently have over a *50 percent positive response rate* for the condition for which they thought they were being treated.

Simply the *thought* that one is receiving a potentially effective trial drug or trial surgery can change one's deeply held convictions about one's state of health. As in the cases of MPD sufferers, when the conviction changes, so does the physical body. Placebo-induced change can sometimes happen immediately (as with the placebo inhalers); but it generally unfolds more slowly than do the dramatically rapid changes of MPD sufferers, because the speed of change occurs in accordance with the *mental expectations*, that is, the convictions of the placebo takers. If, for example, there is a deep conviction that they will *gradually* lose all their hair, then they do.

Many in the medical field will argue that there is a purely biochemical explanation for the placebo effect—the brain releases neuropeptides and neurotransmitters in response to the thoughts created inside our physical brain. These chemical messengers flow through our bloodstream delivering their messages to countless cells, thereby triggering the biochemical processes that cause the changes.

Although it is true that neuropeptides and neurotransmitters are constantly being released by the neurons in the brain, and that the purpose of their release is to alter body chemistry, there is a strong counterargument to explain why their effect does not eliminate the need for a more subtle explanation of the placebo effect: Neuropeptides and neurotransmitters stimulating known biochemical processes cannot come close to explaining the speed at which MPD sufferers undergo physiological change.

There are yet more reasons to accept the power of our thoughts: We have more than ample proof that our thoughts can affect the thoughts of other people—*telepathy*—and our thoughts can affect matter outside our physical body—*telekinesis*.

Thousands of studies confirm the reality of telepathy and telekinesis. Even though mainstream science has difficulty accepting the studies' results, there really is no question that our thoughts can effect matter as well as interact with the thoughts of others. Various experiments conducted in hundreds of laboratories around the world—including those at Stanford University and the once affiliated Stanford Research Institute (SRI), Duke University's Rhine Institute, Princeton's PEAR, Cornell University, the Institute of Noetic Sciences, and the CIA's Stargate labs—provide scientifically and meticulously gathered results that confirm the existence of such phenomena.

If you have doubts that such studies have confirmed that thought exists outside the brain and can affect the thoughts of other people as well as matter, I recommend that you read Dean Radin's book, _Entangled Minds_. Dr. Radin is currently chief scientist at the Institute of Noetic Sciences (IONS). Before joining the research staff at IONS in 2001, he held appointments at AT&T Bell Labs, Princeton University, University of Edinburgh, and SRI International. In _Entangled Minds_, he describes in detail the extra-exacting methodologies modern studies on thought and consciousness have been forced to use in order to combat the accusations of fraud and sloppy science that have been leveled against such studies for the last hundred years. And he shares the results of several meta-analyses conducted by his team as well as other meta-analyses conducted by other research teams around the world. Meta-analysis is a discipline used in many conventional disciplines: By combining the data from hundreds—and in many cases thousands—of tests, meta-analysis can amplify very small effects that otherwise would not be possible to measure and can methodically weed out statistical problems that skew results due to lack of scientific rigor such as underreporting failed experiments.

Here are the highlights from the meta-analysis of two simple but telling types of experiments: Dozens of experiments—performed in multiple labs by different teams over the course of many decades—have conducted thousands of trials to see whether people can tell if they are being stared at. (That people _can_ tell if they are being stared at is a widely held belief.) To test this theory, researchers place subjects in a room shielded from all electromagnetic, sound, and vibrational influence. They cannot see, hear, feel, or communicate with anyone. There is no normal way they can directly sense the presence of a starer. The subjects are prompted at regular intervals to indicate whether they think someone has been staring at them. Sometimes someone is staring at them and sometimes no one is staring at them. The actual staring occurs according to a randomly selected pattern.

If it were the case that staring at someone had no effect whatsoever on the person being stared at, then the subjects' answers would be purely guesswork and, averaged over thousands of trials, would conform to pure chance—50 percent of the time they would be right, and 50 percent of the time they would be wrong or very close to it. Instead, the subjects correctly indicated when they were being stared at—averaged over the course of 33,357 trials—54.5 percent of the time.

Although it may not seem like much, a deviation from a 50/50 distribution of 4.5 percent in more than 30,000 trials is immensely, gigantically significant. If a coin-flipping machine flips a fair coin 33,357 times, the trial tally would be very close to 50 percent heads and 50 percent tails—every single time the experiment is run. And every single time the experiment is run with more than 30,000 flips—even if you run a million 30,000-flip experiments—the result will *always* conform to results consistent with chance, with approximately 50 percent heads and 50 percent tails. If staring had no effect on the one being stared at, the outcome over 33,357 tests would with statistical certainty be a 50/50 distribution of correct/incorrect guesses. The astonishing odds against there being a 4.5 percent deviation from a 50/50 distribution in these experiments are 10^{46} to 1.[4]

Another simple experiment has also been conducted thousands of times: Subjects are asked to influence the throw of dice. The meta-analysis cited in *Entangled Minds* examined the results of a combined total of 2,500 people trying to influence the outcome of more than 2.6 million throws of the dice. Again, if it really is impossible for people to influence the outcome of a throw, then the results would conform to pure chance. But they didn't. The results skewed a few percentage points outside the expected distribution pattern. Again, a very small effect, but the odds against the results straying from pure chance is 10^{76} to 1.[5]

Similarly mind-boggling meta-analytical statistics have been compiled from experiments testing the ability of people telepathically sending and receiving images from mind to mind, successfully performing remote viewing, and telekinetically influencing the outcome of such highly controlled and randomly generated physical and electronic systems as were used in the PEAR experiments described in Chapter 1.

The statistics overwhelmingly indicate that there is *absolutely no question* that people have the telepathic ability to receive thoughts from and send thoughts to others, and telekinetically to affect matter. Forget fraud, forget bias, forget sloppy science; those accusations just don't wash. It's simply not possible to explain away *all* of these carefully observed phenomena.

Why then does mainstream science not accept these results?

The problem for mainstream scientists is that no one has yet found an energy, or a substance, or a field, or a *measureable something* that, under observation in an experimental framework, will explain the effect of thought on matter, or how thought can exist beyond the brain. Yet the data clearly indicates that thought and consciousness *do* exist outside the brain and *can* effect matter.

Scientific materialists are left in a quandary—unable to refute the evidence but unwilling to embrace it. Many may share the thinking of Professor Richard Wiseman, a psychologist at the University of Hertfordshire and a leading skeptic regarding anything paranormal, who was quoted in an article appearing in Britain's *Daily Mail*:

> I agree that by the standards of any other area of science that remote viewing is proven but begs the question: do we need higher standards of evidence when we study the paranormal? Because remote viewing is such an outlandish claim that will revolutionise the world, we need overwhelming evidence. . . .[6]

The quandary scientific materialists face is greatly intensified when quantum physics is added to the discussion. While the scientific materialists, by sheer dint of not wanting it to be true, have pushed to the fringe anything "paranormal," such as telepathy and telekinesis, they have, for nearly 100 years, been unable to explain away quantum physics' oft-demonstrated need for an intelligent observer in the formation of matter. The result has remained a glaring inconsistency in scientific materialism's argument that thought is created by and confined to biochemical processes taking place *inside* the physical brain.

I won't assume you remember the description and implication of the intelligent-observer paradox. Let me briefly recap using the same diagrams you have already seen in Chapter 1:

1. Electromagnetic energy, which includes visible light, can behave as a wave or as a stream of particles, a phenomenon known as *wave-particle duality*. Counterintuitively, *matter* exhibits wave-particle duality as well. What we think of as matter, and therefore as being made up of particles, nonetheless can also behave as a wave. Thus physicists tend to use the term *matter-wave* to avoiding having to say whether something is in a wave or particle form since, depending on the situation, it could be either one.

2. According to the results of countless experiments, matter—if unmeasured, or unobserved by an intelligent observer—will remain in a wave state. Only when measured by an intelligent observer will it behave as particles.

3. Experiments have shown that light moving through double slits will generate an interference pattern characteristic of how waves of *any* kind, from light waves to water waves, interfere with each other (Figure 11).

4. When individual photons (the particle form of light) were sent through the double slits one at a time, the experimenters naturally expected to see no interference pattern at all. They expected to see two vertical collections of photon impacts on the detector, collections that would form a pattern like bullets fired through such slits into a target. Instead, and to their astonishment, they still saw an *interference* pattern (Figure 12).

5. How could this be? How could an individual photon, a particle, interfere with anything if it is the only thing going

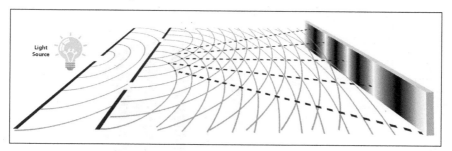

FIGURE 11. *The characteristic pattern of waves interfering with each other occurs when light shines through double slits and strikes a detector on the other side. Where crests meet crests or troughs meet troughs the waves are amplified (the bright detector lines on the right); where crests meet troughs the waves are nullified (the dark detector lines on the right).*

through the slits? Other experiments were eventually conducted in which a measuring device was placed by the slits to detect which slit an individual photon actually traveled through. (The measuring device does not interfere in any way with the passage of the photons through the slits.) Once the measuring device was added to the experiment, the photons passed through the slits and hit the detector with the same pattern as would bullets fired from a gun (Figure 13).

Do you hear the *Twilight Zone* theme again?

As described in Chapter 1, the *only difference* in the two experimental setups was that the passage of the photons through the slits had been *measured by an intelligent observer*. Scientists have conducted essentially this same experiment time and again without finding the counterintuitive outcome to be a result of a flaw in the procedure. No matter how many times it has been done, and no matter how much the scientists conducting the experiment might want there to be another outcome, the results are always the same: Measurement by an intelligent observer always causes the matter-wave to behave like matter—and in the absence of such a measurement, the matter-wave behaves like a wave.

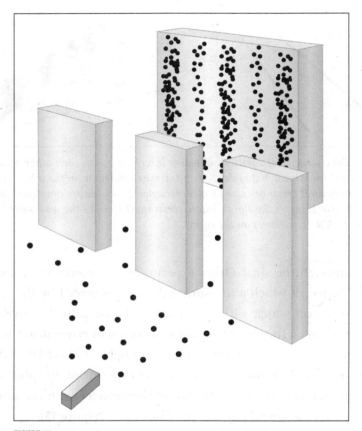

FIGURE 12. *What they actually saw, even though photons were sent one at a time through the slits, was the same interference pattern one sees in Figure 11. The interference pattern formed by single photons is a little rougher than the interference pattern created by a continuous light source, but is unmistakably the same pattern.*

We are left with the fact that an intelligent observer is—somehow—integral to the formation of matter.

As mentioned in previous chapters, the search for a solution to the paradoxical result of measurement by an intelligent observer, and other "quantum weirdness," has spawned among physicists a number of interpretations of quantum physics. The Copenhagen interpretation, touched on earlier, can be thought of as the pragmatic shut-up-and-calculate interpretation. "Don't worry about a *deeper* reality. It's not necessary. This is just the way things work. Matter becomes weird at quantum size. Get used to it." Although the pragmatic Copenhagen interpretation stays afloat on the sea of scientific materialism by not rocking the boat with nonmaterial speculations, it does not answer the abiding question: *Why* is there an intelligent-observer effect? Its pragmatism works, but

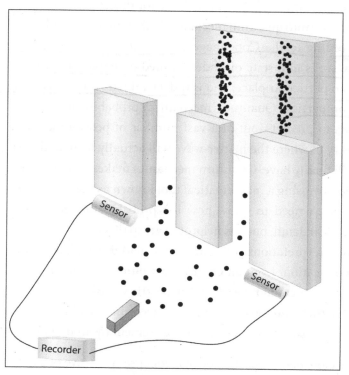

FIGURE 13. *Once the experiment was set up to measure which slit individual photons were passing through, the photons behaved like particles, creating the pattern on the detector one would expect of little bits of matter.*

it doesn't satisfy, and, in fact, for decades allegiance to the Copenhagen interpretation has been declining.[7]

A newer interpretation, one that appeals especially to scientific materialists and that has attracted popular interest as well, is the many-worlds interpretation (MWI). The many-worlds interpretation is particularly attractive to scientific materialists because it offers the possibility to *eliminate altogether the need for an intelligent observer.* MWI posits that it only *appears* to us that an intelligent observer is necessary to cause the matter-wave to take on its particle form while, in fact, there is no intelligent-observer effect at all.

To understand how the MWI allows for this conclusion, we need to go a little further into quantum mechanics' inherently probabilistic approach.

According to the Copenhagen and many other interpretations, the matter-wave is in a state of undetermined potential: It exists nonlocally, thus in no particular place, and is indeterminate, thus possessing no particular properties. Quantum mechanics' probabilistic approach allows physicists to predict—out of a vast number of possibilities—the highest probability of where the matter-wave will actually form and what properties it will finally have. Quantum mechanics makes its highest-probability prediction by using a mathematical tool known as the *waveform.*

You don't need to know how the probabilistic waveform works in mathematical detail, but it is helpful to grasp this core concept: According to many interpretations, the moment a matter-wave takes on a specific form and location, from among the vast number of other possible forms and locations it could take, the probabilistic waveform is said to have *collapsed.* Further, and most significantly, according to almost all interpretations, what causes it to collapse is measurement by an intelligent observer.

> Consciousness is the agency that collapses the wave of a quantum object.
>
> —Amit Goswami, quantum physicist[8]

The shorthand way of expressing this axiom is that measurement by an intelligent observer *collapses the waveform*. No observer, no collapse; no observer, no matter.

If this axiom is true, if some still unmeasured influence emanating from the intelligent observer causes the waveform to collapse, then scientific materialism does not provide a full explanation of the cosmos. The presence of such an influence would mean that matter and energy do not make up all there is or ever will be—that there is something else beyond matter and energy. And, because the intelligent-observer paradox strongly suggests that scientific materialism is fundamentally incomplete, we can understand why adherents of scientific materialism have fallen on the many-worlds interpretation with gladsome cries: They believe they've found a strictly interacting matter- and energy-based answer to the intelligent-observer paradox.

Here's their answer: According to MWI, *every one of the vast number of possibilities*—of where and in what form a matter-wave could manifest—*actually do manifest*. MWI's adherents posit that although it appears to *us* that only one possibility manifested, and that therefore there was a *single* waveform collapse manifesting a single outcome, in fact *all* the other possibilities *also* manifested, and that, when they did, they caused our universe to branch into as many new universes as there were possibilities.

Got that? MWI theorizes that every possibility manifests—no matter how improbable—and that in the moment of manifesting, each possibility causes the *entire universe* to branch or bud into an entirely new, separate, and nearly identical universe.

According to MWI, our universe of the moment, and all the other universes that have already branched before it, and those that will branch after it, will all continue to branch into yet more universes as new sets of quantum possibilities arise in each universe. In infinitesimally short order, the number of universes created becomes indescribably large: 10 to the trillionth? Oops, now it's 10 to the quadrillionth, and so on and on.

Numbers like 10 to the $10^{10,000,000\text{th}}$ are used to describe the number of separate universes that could exist.

It's a rather profligate theory to say the least.

In addition to apparently avoiding any need for an intelligent observer—with its associated and pesky issues of consciousness—MWI also appears to solve for scientific materialists what is called the Goldilocks-universe problem. As mentioned in a previous chapter, it has been convincingly argued that hundreds of conditions—from the absolutely precise strength of gravity to the existence of an excited state of carbon-12 called the Hoyle State—all have to be *just right*, like Goldilocks's porridge, in order for our universe to unfold as it did and for life to arise within it.

The many-worlds interpretation gives scientific materialists a way around the Goldilocks problem, as well as around the intelligent-observer paradox. Scientific materialists apply Darwinian thinking to the ever-branching, many-worlds concept. They reason that because so many zillions of universes branch and change, it was *inevitable* that at least one would pop into existence with the exact conditions necessary for life. •

There are, however, fundamental problems with the many-worlds approach. While MWI avoids the intelligent-observer paradox and the Goldilocks-universe problem, it creates a gigantic problem of *causation*. Proponents propose that every *possibility*, however unlikely and however insignificant, has sufficient causal power to create an entire universe. For the many-worlds interpretation to be valid, a nebulous, indefinable, and unmeasurable quantity—possibility—must have infinite power of causation.

On the human side of things, MWI is completely nihilistic. It proposes absolute meaninglessness. Everything that possibly could happen, happens. In my universe of the moment, I keep writing this sentence, while in the zillion other universes where some version of me exists, I do other things. In some universe, Hitler became the good guy and the Allies were the oppressors. In some universe, Jesus stayed a carpenter. In some universe, Beethoven was tone deaf and Einstein was an idiot. In some universe, Rush Limbaugh is president. In some universe, *I* am president. In some universe, I was killed by my mother. In some universe, I killed my mother. In some universe, we live like savages. In some universe, we live like saints. In most universes, there is no life at all and intelligence never arises.

According to the many-worlds interpretation, I might think I'm seeing logical outcomes to the choices I make, but I'm not; instead, *every* possibility is manifested. I, here in my universe of the moment, am aware only of one outcome and therefore think that that outcome is the result of my prior actions. In MWI, there is no correlation at all between action and result, cause and effect. Causality is thrown out the window. There is no self-determination. Nothing you do makes any difference. You are not an individual but rather a fleetingly momentary collection of accidentally combined possibilities. In MWI, the protean energy-verse randomly spews forth physical universes like a perpetually erupting volcano governed by neither evolution nor purpose.

MWI is the ultimate expression of scientific materialism's belief that all things are the result of matter-energy interactions and random chance. With all due respect, you MWI guys can keep your theory.

While the Copenhagen, the many-worlds, and a handful of other quantum physics' interpretations stay within the bounds of scientific materialism, there *are* other equally reputable interpretations that *go beyond* the limitations of scientific materialism. These other interpretations embrace the possibility that the intelligent-observer effect indicates that there is more to reality than scientific materialism's matter-energy interactions. They embrace the idea that thought and consciousness have an existence independent of matter and energy.

The most well-known among the interpretations that embrace a fundamental role for thought and consciousness is attributed to a group of eminent physicists whose contributions were central to the development of quantum physics—John von Neumann, John Archibald Wheeler, and Eugene Wigner; among them they possess a Nobel Prize and nearly every other award that has ever been given to physicists. Their shared interpretation is known rather lengthily as the von Neumann–Wheeler–Wigner interpretation (vNWWI). It rests on the premise that thought and consciousness are not just fleeting artifacts of the biochemical processes of the brain; rather, thought and consciousness are the *fundamental causative elements of the cosmos.*

You could say vNWWI is the polar opposite of scientific materialism: It posits not only that thought and consciousness exist beyond matter, but that thought and consciousness *create* matter.

The many eminent proponents of vNWWI and other interpretations that embrace thought and consciousness at times sound more like philosophers and mystics than scientists:

It was not possible to formulate the laws (of quantum theory) in a fully consistent way without reference to consciousness.
> —Eugene Wigner, Nobel Prize winner in physics[9]

There is obviously only one alternative, namely the unification of minds . . . [I]n truth there is only one mind.
> —Erwin Schrödinger, Nobel Prize winner in physics[10]

"Observership" is a prerequisite for any useful version of "reality."
> —John Archibald Wheeler, prize-winning physicist[11]

I would say that in my scientific and philosophical work, my main concern has been with understanding the nature of reality in general and of consciousness in particular as a coherent whole.
> —David Bohm, Fellow of the Royal Society[12]

Consciousness is the crux of the physics of God: It is in consciousness that science and religion come together, and it is through an understanding of consciousness that we can reconcile the apparent conflicts between them. Acceptance of consciousness as the foundation of the cosmos, however, does not come easily.

If you are not yet familiar with vNWWI's approach to consciousness, you may well find it baffling or unsettling—or both. You are not alone. Though endorsed by great scientific minds, though amply supported by mathematics, though there is no other proven explanation for the intelligent-observer effect, most physicists and scientists, in a very human way, *viscerally* reject the notion that something as seemingly ephemeral as consciousness could be the foundation of reality.

The idea that consciousness is the foundation of reality threatens most people's bedrock experiential worldview. It's not so much that the implications of vNWWI are counterintuitive (a term often used to describe quantum physics), as it is that the implications are *countersensory.*

What we experience through the senses suggests that everything around us has an independent and separate material reality. Gravity acts on a glass when we drop it. The glass breaks into pieces when it hits the floor. Nothing else is affected. Other glasses still on the counter do not break. The floor does not shatter. The glass that was an independent object is now a pile of smaller independent objects.

Though my example is simplistic, it captures the essence of our continuous sensory experience of how the world works. It is easy, therefore, to see why scientists, and indeed, most people, naturally want to extend their everyday sense-provided experience of the things in their life to everything that exists: There was a Big Bang. Little independent entities we call atoms formed. The independent atoms formed into independent stars and planets. Our planet gave rise to independent lifeforms.

Such a view of reality is comfortable and natural because it is an extension of our everyday perceptions. It is emotionally comfortable, and it *is* true to an extent—it just doesn't tell the whole story.

We saw in Chapter 3 that the reality we perceive through the senses is very limited. Our senses can only perceive a tiny band of the spectrum of vibrating energies within which we exist like fish in the sea. In our day-to-day, sense-revealed existence, we are mostly blind. We cannot sensorily perceive the sea of energy interpenetrating our physical bodies that connects us to everything.

> A human being is a part of the whole, called by us universe, a part limited in time and space. He experiences himself, his thoughts and feeling as something separate from the rest—a kind of optical delusion of his consciousness.
>
> —Albert Einstein[13]

> The existing scientific concepts cover always only a very limited part of reality, and the other part that has not yet been understood is infinite.
>
> —Werner Heisenberg, Nobel Prize–winning physicist[14]

If our senses were able to reveal all of the vibrating sea of energy in which we exist, we would know that no atom has inherent, enduring, independent properties. It is simply energy; energy that can take any form. String theorists add that the apparently independent objects that make up our sensory experience are super-high resolution, three-dimensional images in a holographic projection. Just as the images on our TV screen appear to be separate and independently existing three-dimensional objects, they are in fact interconnected, two-dimensional light images. So, too, the world around us, and indeed our bodies, are holographic projections of energy—not separate, independently existing three-dimensional objects. Neither the tiniest bit of matter nor the largest star has an independent reality. All matter is projected from, interconnected with, and dependent on, the interpenetrating, nonlocal, two-dimensional energy-verse.

Once we accept that quantum physics' and string theory's laws and insights (highlighted in the previous paragraph) provide a truer description of reality than what our senses can reveal, it is perhaps less difficult to make the leap of understanding that intelligent consciousness also exists nonlocally in the same way as do the energies of the energy-verse.

My conclusion is that consciousness is not a thing or substance, but is a nonlocal phenomenon. Nonlocal is merely a fancy word for infinite. If something is nonlocal, it is not localized to specific points in space, such as brains or bodies, or to specific points in time, such as the present. Nonlocal events are immediate; they require no travel time. They are unmediated; they require no energetic signal to "carry" them. They are unmitigated; they do not become weaker with increasing distance. Nonlocal phenomena are omnipresent, everywhere at once. This means there is no necessity for them to go anywhere; they are already there. They are infinite in time as well, present at all moments, past present and future, meaning they are eternal.

—Larry Dossey, author of *The Science of Premonitions*[15]

I regard consciousness as fundamental. I regard matter as a derivative of consciousness. We cannot get behind consciousness. Everything that we talk about, everything that we regard as existing, [suggests] consciousness.

—Max Planck, Nobel Prize winner in physics[16]

The stream of knowledge is heading toward a non-mechanical reality; the universe begins to look more like a great thought than like a great machine. Mind no longer appears to be an accidental intruder into the realm of matter, we ought rather hail it as the creator and governor of the realm of matter. Get over it, and accept the inarguable conclusion. The universe is immaterial-mental and spiritual.

—Sir James Jeans, physicist[17]

I have concluded that we are in a world made by rules created by an intelligence. To me it is clear that we exist in a plan which is governed by rules that were created, shaped by a universal intelligence and not by chance.

—Michio Kaku, string theorist[18]

What these physicists glimpse—and what the saints and sages understand—is that the universe and the laws that guide it in all its intricate detail spring from a dimensionless foundation of intelligent consciousness.

Intelligent consciousness is the director and producer of the cosmic movie.

> The cosmic cinema is a glorious manifestation of the imaginary thought processes of God's Mind, but the projected light images of God's imagining, which seem to move and have life of being in themselves, are but electrically-sensed thought forms of thought imaginings that but constitute a mirage of the reality which they but simulate.
>
> —Walter Russell, sculptor, musician, author,
> philosopher, and mystic[19]

Using television as an analogy, the picture we enjoy seeing, the progression of the storyline with characters acting out a script, is but a trick of perception. Your mind connects the electron/ dots into the picture images you think you see, while it totally ignores the true reality of what actually undergirds the operation. Existence is a lot like television. What exists, what really exists, can't be fathomed by how it appears to operate or what it seems to be.

> —P.M.H. Atwater, author of *Beyond the Light*[20]

The "cosmic motion picture" is true not only to two human senses, sight and hearing, but to all five. It is presented to us three-dimensionally and includes the illusion of smell, taste, and touch. And yet, just as the light emanating from the projection booth produces mere images of reality, so also does God's light produce mere appearances.

> —Swami Kriyananda, author of *Essence of the Bhagavad Gita*[21]

As Sir James Jeans urges us, if we are to reconcile the transcendent revelations of the saints and sages with science, we need to "get over it, and accept the inarguable conclusion. The universe is immaterial-mental and spiritual."[22] Without embracing consciousness as the nonlocal foundation of the cosmos, the transcendent revelations of the saints and sages are impossible to explain.

Fortunately, we do not need to "get over it, and accept the inarguable conclusion" without rational scientific support. In addition to Sir James Jeans, scores of eminent scientists have accepted the cosmos's nonmaterial foundation in consciousness. And if, like me, you are also deeply persuaded by the consistency and certainty of the testimony of the thousands of saints, sages, and near-death experiencers who have had transcendent experiences, then their testimony that reality is a cosmic movie, a light-show illusion—supported scientifically by the holographic principle and the vNWW interpretation that consciousness is the foundation of reality—provides a clear path fully to reconcile the obvious truths of science and the obvious truths of religion.

Science and religion find their common ground in consciousness.

The light-show illusion that is our physical universe is continuously created by the energy-verse; in turn, the laws that inform the energy-verse's continuous creation of the physical universe spring from infinite, nonlocal, intelligent consciousness. The screenplay for the cosmic movie, the two-dimensional holographic system that projects the cosmic movie, and the resulting light-show illusion—the three-dimensional, cosmic movie—all spring from and are guided by intelligent consciousness.

CHAPTER 8

"Ye Are Gods"

The physics of God has enormous significance for us as individuals.

We inhabit simultaneously our local three-dimensional physical bodies and our nonlocal interpenetrating, two-dimensional energy bodies. When we feel our life force, our vitality, we are feeling the subtle energies of our interpenetrating, nonlocal two-dimensional energy bodies.

Most of what we are exists beyond the physical universe.

Our local, three-dimensional physical bodies are the holographic projections of our nonlocal, two-dimensional holographic energy bodies. Our two-dimensional energy bodies are the source of most of what we experience as ourselves—our awareness, feelings, motivations, memories, and life-energy.

We cannot truly die.

Our three-dimensional physical body allows us to exist in the three-dimensional physical world of space, time, and matter—like a deep-sea diver wearing a suit that allows him to survive deep underwater. When we die, our space, time, and matter suit ceases to function, and we are no longer able to operate in space, time, and matter. When we die our awareness shifts to our nonlocal, two-dimensional energy body in the energy-verse.

What we think—we become.

Our nonlocal, intelligent consciousness *shapes* our nonlocal, two-dimensional holographic energy template. Our nonlocal, two-dimensional holographic energy template, in turn, shapes our physical body. Our local, three-dimensional physical body is continuously sustained and controlled by our nonlocal, shaped-by-thought two-dimensional energy body via the bridge of quantum entanglement.

Our deeply held thoughts are powerful.

We see this power in the placebo effect; it is even more dramatically demonstrated in the nearly instantaneous physiological changes of MPD sufferers. Every moment of every day, the holographic projection we experience as our physical bodies manifests *exactly* what our deeply held thoughts dictate. The moment we change such deeply held thoughts is the moment our physical body changes.

We are even more amazing: We *make* the world.

Without intelligent observers—*us*—the cosmic movie, the light-show illusion of matter, *will not play.* The intelligent-observer effect has been painstakingly and exactly measured, and confirmed, in thousands of double-slit experiments. One might be tempted to dismiss the double-slit experiments as parlor tricks that affect only a few miniscule photons or atoms, but the implication of the intelligent-observer effect is profound: Without intelligent observers, there can be no world.

The universe and the observer exist as a pair.

—Andrei Linde, Stanford University physicist[1]

This is a *participatory* universe.

—John Archibald Wheeler, prize-winning physicist[2]

There is no object in space-time without a conscious subject looking at it.

—Amit Goswami, quantum physicist[3]

We are what we think, all that we are arises with our thoughts, with our thoughts we make the world.

—Buddha[4]

I would not be surprised if you find it hard to accept that you are essential to the existence of the physical universe, that you "make the world." "It's just there," you probably think, "and I have nothing to do with it!" Yet our essential role in the existence of the physical universe has been confirmed over and over by science's intelligent-observer experiments— *a matter wave only behaves like matter when observed by an intelligent observer.*

You are not alone if you find this concept difficult to grasp. Einstein famously said, "I'd like to think the moon is still there even when I am not looking at it." Indeed, most people find it unsettling to think that we play *any* role in matter's manifestation. The idea that everything requires someone's attention lest it wink out of existence seems a recipe for chaos. One might think that a person could unknowingly and randomly cause *different* things to manifest than the person before: Where there had been a chair there is now a table; where there had been a dog there is now a cat; where there had been a car there is now a house. If such were true, our daily experience would be a chance-driven Mad Hatter's tea party.

Yet our daily experience is the opposite of the Mad Hatter's tea party. We experience a stable physical world that behaves according to consistent natural laws. If, for example, you go down into a basement that no one "observes" but you, all the items will be unmoved since your last visit. Items will have gathered dust. Water from a problem leak will have seeped onto the floor, causing mold to grow. Items will have decayed in small ways or large depending on how durable the object and how long since your last visit. In other words, the basement—despite you not having been there to observe it—will have changed according to natural laws over which you have no conscious control. You will have every reason to believe that your basement has led a *separate* existence, independent of you or your observation of it. Good Question!

How, then, do we reconcile our day-to-day experience of an enduring, consistent, independent, and stable physical reality with the idea that the physical world can't exist without us? If it requires an intelligent observer to bring matter into manifestation, then why does matter always change with the passage of time and according to the effects of natural laws? How can both be true?

The answer is that the origin of the physical world's lawful consistency is in *the hidden mechanism that plays the cosmic movie*: the nonlocal, two-dimensional holographic energy template that creates and sustains the physical universe. The nonlocal, two-dimensional holographic energy template, like film in a projector, contains all the information to project the cosmic movie we know as the physical universe.

The nonlocal, two-dimensional holographic energy template can be thought of in terms of Bohm's *implicate order*, which contains the "hidden properties" that determine how individual matter waves manifest in the *explicate order* (the three-dimensional physical world). Or we can think of the nonlocal, two-dimensional holographic energy template as containing the heavens, and of the heavens as the hologram from which the three-dimensional universe takes its form. Yet another way to understand the universe's nonlocal, holographic energy template is to think of it as an organized collection of *matter waves* imperceptible to our senses, which requires an intelligent observer to make the matter waves behave as matter.

Unlike film in a projector, the holographic energy template isn't fixed or static; it is dynamically evolving in accordance with its own inherent, intelligently created laws—more like a computer program than like a film. The old computer game SimCity could run a simulation of how a city would evolve over years, decades, and even centuries because its programming contained the basic laws that governed the outcome. The holographic energy template, likewise, contains the laws that govern all matter-energy interactions and contains all the information about the evolving state of the physical universe—the complete history of all matter-energy interactions from the Big Bang to the present.

The universe's nonlocal, holographic energy template—whether you consider it in Bohmian terms, heavenly terms, as an organized collection of matter waves, or as the ultimate SimCity—is continuously running and program-like; it keeps lawfully evolving and organizing all the matter waves that compose it—no matter how much time passes between observations by an intelligent observer.

When we intelligent observers *do* observe a particular matter wave or collection of matter waves, our observation *causes* those particular matter waves to behave as matter, but in a way that is already predetermined: The matter waves' hidden properties, the energy template's inherent laws, the cosmic movie's hidden scripts, predetermine the specific form the matter wave will take.

Thus, random intelligent observations do *not* result in chaos. When Einstein looked at the moon, it was "still there" as Einstein would like to have believed, its cosmic holographic program still determining how it spins on its axis and lawfully evolves, but it would not have behaved as perceptible matter unless Einstein or someone else was observing it.

The physical world's lawful consistency is assured by its computer program–like holographic energy template. The continuously playing, not-perceptible-to-the-senses, two-dimensional cosmic movie—what a saint once called, "God's super-colossal entertainment"—takes on the form of matter and becomes *perceptible to the senses* when observed by an intelligent observer, but the intelligent observation does not determine the form that matter takes.

However, the cosmic movie's change from sensory imperceptibility to sensory perceptibility is not simply *subjective*. It is *objective*. The double-slit experiments use scientific devices to measure the matter waves' behavior *objectively*. The behavior measured is not simply an individual's subjective point of view. We know objectively that intelligent observers *cause* sensorily imperceptible matter waves to behave as sensorily perceptible matter. To me, and to many others before me, only one conclusion seems possible: *If there were no intelligent observers in the physical universe, the physical universe would cease to exist.*

If the Twilight Zone music would help, feel free to turn it on—but you might want to save it for what's still to come.

Almost all of us have no conscious awareness of our ability to *make* the cosmic movie play in three-dimensions, or to shape our bodies in accordance with our deeply held thoughts. A rare few, however, are consciously aware of these abilities and have learned how to use them deliberately. The rare few are the saints and sages, and they assure us that we, too, can do the same.

> Jesus answered them, Is it not written in your law, I said, Ye are gods?
>
> —John 10:34

> Very truly I tell you, whoever believes in me will do the works I have been doing, and they will do even greater things than these.
>
> —John 14:12

> Since everything is made out of mind, it can be controlled by mind. As you develop more and more mental strength, ultimately you will be able to do anything.
>
> —Paramhansa Yogananda, yoga master[5]

One of the timeless claims of religions is that saints and sages can, seemingly, defy the laws of matter: change water into wine, cure the sick, raise the dead, walk on water, levitate, manifest objects out of thin air. However, as I hope you are now able to appreciate, miracles do not defy the laws of matter; rather, they demonstrate deeper laws that science has not yet grasped.

What we think of as miracles are simply the conscious extension of the power we use continuously to shape our own physical bodies and the power we use to cause matter waves to behave as matter. The saints and sages have learned to control the thoughts that shape the matter around them as well as the matter that makes up their own bodies. Not only have the saints and sages learned to change the health and appearance of the body-costume they are wearing in the cosmic movie, *they have learned to change the cosmic movie itself.*

> Through a master's divine knowledge of light phenomena, he can instantly project into perceptible manifestation the ubiquitous light atoms. The actual form of the projection—whether it be a tree, a medicine, a human body—is in conformance with [his] powers of will and of visualization.
>
> —Paramhansa Yogananda, yoga master[6]

This ability, whether hidden or miraculous, is innate in everyone: Everyone possesses the same creative power as does the infinite intelligent consciousness that creates the cosmos.

This central truth lies at the heart of all religions: We are divine children of God, made in His formless, infinite image, inseparable from His consciousness. Like the children of all parents, we possess the abilities of our divine parent.

In Genesis (1:27), we read that God made man in his image, a statement nearly always taken to mean that God has a physical form like *our* physical form. But the opposite is meant. The real "image" of God is infinite consciousness—*that* is the image in which we are made—we come from, are part of, and share, infinite intelligent consciousness.

The teachings of India include this well-known dictum: "atman is Brahman"—the atman (soul) is Brahman (God). The New Testament records Jesus saying: "I and my Father are one" (John: 10:30). The Buddhists tell us we are all One:

> The creative power of the universe is not a human being; it is Buddha. The one who sees, and the one who hears, is not this eye or ear, but the one who is *this* consciousness. *This One* is Buddha. *This One* appears in every mind. *This One* is common to all sentient beings, and is God.[7]

We are gods with amnesia.

Near-death experiencer Jan Price says, "Born of God, we are spirit, and cannot be anything else. All is mind—one mind. We are that mind asleep—yet awakening, and God is that mind eternally aware."[8]

Jesus said, "Lest ye see signs and wonders ye will not believe" (John 4:48). Miracles, though fascinating and inspiring, are only performed by saints and sages to awaken belief. The miracles of the saints and sages are strong prods to our sleeping memories of our divine nature. Their purpose is not to entice us to want to perform miracles ourselves, but to awaken us to our divine potential, to shake us out of our amnesia-induced conviction that we are merely physical bodies and that this physically manifesting cosmic movie is the only reality.

Even when we realize we have amnesia, however, even when we believe in the power of our own thought, we will not be immediately able to use its power consciously. Not until we have mastered the exacting mental discipline practiced by the saints and sages will we, like these great ones, be able consciously to use our thoughts to change the hidden, nonlocal energy template and thus the physical world.

Further, our existing convictions run deep into our nonlocal subconscious. Merely thinking with the conscious mind that one has blue eyes instead of brown is not going to overcome the much more powerful conviction—lying deep, and all but inaccessible, in the nonlocal subconscious mind—that one has brown eyes.

We hold our convictions so deeply that even when they make us miserable we cannot easily change them. Being told that a problem is all in the mind is no help at all—as a wise man said, "That's jolly well the worst place for it to be." Our deeply held thoughts are like girders that hold together the structure of our being. And like steel girders, our thought girders are immensely strong.

The exacting discipline undergone by the saints and sages to achieve such profound mental control begins with direct experience of one's subtle, nonmaterial, divine nature. Intellectual belief in our higher potential, our divine nature, is a starting point, but belief is not enough to change deeply held convictions that the physical world is fixed, immutable, and separate from ourselves. Direct inner experience attained through practicing the disciplines of the science of religion, on the other hand, will transmute those deeply held convictions of materiality by enabling us directly to experience the subtler, interconnected, nonmaterial reality of energy and thought.

Imagine living your entire life in a spaceship with gravity merely a concept. You may *believe* that gravity exists, but until you visit a planet and directly experience gravity pressing you to the ground, you would be unlikely to be *convinced* that gravity exists. Direct experience attained by practicing the science of religion overcomes the *conviction* of materiality. The saints and sages, who are just as aware of their subtle divine nature as we are aware of our physical bodies, know that their energy-body template and the thoughts that shape it have an independent transcendent reality; theirs is not belief, it is *knowing*. And with knowing comes the ability to shape the thoughts that shape physical form—the ability to perform what are commonly called "miracles."

Miraculous abilities are, however, only a sideshow. The greatest ability we possess is the ability to *turn off* the cosmic movie. We turn on the cosmic movie by perceiving through the senses; we turn off the cosmic movie by transcending the senses. When one achieves perfect stillness and profound inner absorption through meditation, one's awareness becomes vastly expanded until finally one can perceive the vast cosmos beyond the physical universe.

Our physical bodies, like the costumes of actors on a stage, are part of the cosmic movie. But just as costumed actors are not their costumes, we are not our bodies. Our bodies are three-dimensional costumes we need to wear to play our parts on this three-dimensional stage. And, as actors, the parts we play are only a small part of who and what we are. We simultaneously exist within and beyond this physical world. Our consciousness is nonlocal, essentially infinite, and like the high-frequency energies of our energy body; it exists beyond, yet interpenetrates, our physical bodies.

With expanded perception comes freedom from the limitations of the body. The experience bestows a profound sense of joyous well-being, "beyond imagination of expectancy," and undeniably clear awareness of one's indissoluble unity with the infinite Consciousness from which all creation springs. Some of the names given to this experience are "cosmic consciousness," "samadhi," "oneness," "nirvana," "Christ consciousness," "enlightenment," "self-realization," "divine ecstasy," "rapture," and "union."

This is the experience of God, or, just as meaningfully, the experience of our Self or soul. Because we are *all* Divine in our essence, all inextricably one with God, the experience is not reserved only for cloistered nuns or yogis in remote Himalayan caves. Anyone, anywhere, who achieves deep stillness and complete inner absorption, regardless of how, shares the same universal experience.

A kind of waking trance (this for lack of a better word) I have frequently had quite up from boyhood. When I have been all alone. This has often come upon me through repeating my own name to myself silently, till all at once as it were out of the intensity of the consciousness of individuality the individuality itself seemed to dissolve and fade away into boundless being—and this not a confused state but the clearest of the clearest, the surest of the surest, utterly beyond words—where Death was an almost laughable impossibility—the loss of personality (if so it were) seeming no extinction but the only true life.

—Alfred Lord Tennyson, Poet Laureate of
Great Britain and Ireland[9]

All at once, without warning of any kind, he found himself wrapped around as it were by a flame-coloured cloud . . . he knew that the light was within himself. Directly afterwards came upon him a sense of exaltation, of immense joyousness accompanied or immediately followed by an intellectual illumination quite impossible to describe . . . he saw and knew that the cosmos is not dead matter but a living Presence, that the soul of man is immortal, that the universe is so ordered that without any peradventure all things work together for the good of each and all, that the foundation principle of the world is what we call love.

—Richard Maurice Bucke, speaking in the third-person;
Canadian psychiatrist, author of *Cosmic Consciousness*[10]

The body, the earth, the stars, the galaxies melted into a big unity—and I was a part of this unity. Unlimited and timeless my consciousness hovered in a pulsating eternity.

—Frédéric Lionel, French philosopher[11]

One becomes wholly Mind, the One Mind of God, in which exists all-knowledge, all-power, and all-presence.

—Walter Russell, sculptor, musician, author,
philosopher, and mystic[12]

That light is the very essence, the heart and soul, the all-consuming consummation of ecstatic ecstasy. It is a million suns of compressed love dissolving everything unto itself, annihilating thought and cell, vaporizing humanness and history, into the one great brilliance of all that is and all that ever was and all that ever will be.

You know it's God.

No one has to tell you.

You know.

—P.M.H. Atwater, near-death experiencer[13]

The experience is often and movingly described by the saints and sages of all religions. The following are but a few among hundreds, perhaps thousands, of descriptions:

Oh, wonder of wonders, when I think of the union the soul has with God! He makes the enraptured soul to flee out of herself, for she is no more satisfied with anything that can be named. The spring of Divine Love flows out of the soul and draws her out of herself into the unnamed Being, into her first source, which is God alone.

—Meister Eckhart, German theologian, philosopher, and mystic[14]

This new experience bestows new enlightenment which places the experiencer on a new plane of existence. There is an indescribable feeling of elation and indescribable joy and Bliss. He experiences a sense of universality, a Consciousness of Eternal Life. It is not a mere conviction. He actually feels it.

—Swami Sivananda[15]

In the orison [spiritual communion] of union, the soul is fully awake as regards God, but wholly asleep as regards things of this world and in respect of herself.

—St. Teresa of Avila[16]

To the enlightened man whose consciousness embraces the universe, to him the universe becomes his "body," while the physical body becomes a manifestation of the Universal Mind, his inner vision an expression of the highest reality, and his speech an expression of eternal truth.

—Anagarika Govinda, German-born Tibetan Lama[17]

Whilst the mind is separated from itself, and whilst it is borne away into the secret place of the divine mystery and is surrounded on all sides by the fire of divine love, it is inwardly penetrated and inflamed by this fire, and utterly puts off itself and puts on a divine love: and being conformed to that Beauty which it has beheld, it passes utterly into that other glory.

—Richard of St. Victor[18]

The higher our mind is raised to the contemplation of spiritual things the more it is abstracted from sensible things. But the final term to which contemplation can possibly arrive is the divine substance. Therefore the mind that sees the divine substance must be totally divorced from the bodily senses, either by death or by some rapture.

—St. Thomas Aquinas[19]

Soul and mind instantly lost their physical bondage, and streamed out like a fluid piercing light from my every pore. The flesh was as though dead, yet in my intense awareness I knew that never before had I been fully alive.

—Paramhansa Yogananda, yoga master[20]

String theory suggests that there are vast two-dimensional nonlocal realms of high-frequency energies in which our three-dimensional local physical universe exists: saturated, created, and sustained by those energies. Pioneering physicists Werner Heisenberg, Max Planck, John von Neumann, John Wheeler, Eugene Wigner, and David Bohm, as well as modern physicists Fritjof Capra, Gary Zukav, Amit Goswami, Michio Kaku, and *many* others, suggest that these subtler, nonmaterial realms of energy are in turn saturated, created, and sustained by infinite intelligent consciousness.

The saints and sages go further and tell us that this infinite consciousness is *knowable*—Knowable, Intelligent, and Aware—and that we, too, can experience that infinite consciousness and will *inevitably* experience it. And why? *Because we are inseparably one with it*: "The Atman is Brahman." "I and my father are One."

The possibility of the transcendent experience of Oneness is confirmed again and again, in every age and in every culture, by saints, sages, saviors, and near-death experiencers. Such transcendent experience has inspired the mystical teachings of all religions. Such transcendent experience is the *essence*—and the promise—of all religions.

Lest transcendence seem too high a mountain to climb, the good news, for those who, like me, have yet to master perfect stillness and complete inner absorption, is that practicing the science of religion brings many benefits long before transcendence is reached. The benefits infuse one's entire life: reduced physical and emotional stress, an increased sense of well-being, enhanced clarity of mind, increased vitality, improved health, and deepened compassion and love—to name but a few.

Practice the science of religion regularly and you will discover an inexhaustible well of Joy that will imbue your life with happiness regardless of outer circumstances.

Practice the science of religion more deeply yet and you will discover a loving and intelligent Presence responding to you and sending waves of love and joy coursing through your being.

Practice the science of religion to perfection, attaining perfect stillness and inner absorption, and you will experience that there is no separation between yourself and God.

This is the essential teaching of all religions and the message of all the saints, sages, and saviors who ever lived—and the foundation of the physics of God.

The experimentally confirmed and confounding need for the presence of an intelligent observer in order for the matter-wave to behave like matter is a profound hint, provided by science, that we are far more than physical bodies, far more than biological machines, far more, even, than holographic projections of our energy bodies.

We are one with the infinite intelligent consciousness that creates Reality.

The cosmic movie was made for us. Without us, without our attention, the cosmic movie will not play. As you have already read:

The universe and the observer exist as a pair.

—Andrei Linde, Stanford University physicist[21]

This is a participatory universe.

—John Archibald Wheeler, prize-winning physicist[22]

There is no object in space-time without a conscious subject looking at it.

—Amit Goswami, quantum physicist[23]

With our thoughts we make the world.

—Buddha[24]

All of us use our godlike abilities to shape our costume-bodies—some knowingly, most not. Some of us, the saints and sages, can use their godlike abilities to alter even the movie set itself. But the greatest godlike ability we all possess, and that the saints and sages have perfected, is the power to transcend the senses and to turn off the cosmic movie. Watching the cosmic movie in our three-dimensional bodies using only our limited senses reveals next to nothing of Reality; when we transcend the cosmic movie by attaining perfect stillness and inner absorption, Reality—and our oneness with Reality—is revealed.

CHAPTER 9

The Physics of God: A Summary

This book has covered a lot of ground in eight chapters: It has explored the most expansive theories of science and delved into the most profound teachings of religion, while revealing the compelling connections between them. Although this book is short in length, I hope you will agree that it is long on inspiration and concepts: a journey of the heart and mind, not just a collection of facts. To help you to better assimilate and understand what you've read, I have added a summary, a concise recap of the main points. I've included new quotes along with some of my favorites you've already read.

Two new quotes frame well the essence of this book:

> The first gulp from the glass of natural sciences will turn you into an atheist, but at the bottom of the glass God is waiting for you.
> —Werner Heisenberg, Nobel Prize winner[1]

> From science, then, if it must be so, let man learn the philosophic truth that there is no material universe; its warp and woof is . . . illusion.
>
> —Paramhansa Yogananda, yoga master[2]

Science Is Not Inherently Materialistic

The first gulp from the glass of natural sciences appears to rule out any possibility that religion's essential claims can be true. Scientific materialism's credo that everything that is or ever will be is the result of matter-energy interactions is certainly compelling. Matter-energy interactions do explain so many things. But not everything. Matter-energy interactions alone have yet fully to explain the deepest and most important mysteries: the origin and organization of life, the nature of consciousness, and why an intelligent observer is necessary for matter to take form.

More open-minded scientists, those not wedded to scientific materialism's beliefs, accept that matter-energy interactions alone do not explain all observed phenomena; they have been willing to explore nonmaterial alternative theories, ones that look to thought and intelligent consciousness for answers. We have seen that the expanded vision of these open-minded scientists leaves ample room for religion's most universal claims—miracles, heavenly realms, life after death, personal transcendent experience, immortality of the soul, and God, "waiting at the bottom of the glass."

Beneath Religion's Complexities Lies a Consistent Science

The first gulp from the glass of religion reveals a chaos of contradictory claims. Theological descriptions of fundamental beliefs share little common ground among religions. The outward rituals, practices, teaching stories, and ceremonies of the world's religions appear to be as different from one another as are the cultures and languages found around the world. Sectarian beliefs accentuate divisions and differences. Blind attachment to exclusive dogmas leads to repression, violence, and war.

Deeper study, however, reveals an underlying unity, a unity revealed in the testimony of those who have attained transcendent awareness through the practice of the science of religion. If one looks past the centuries of well-intentioned but unenlightened additions to the world's religions—additions that obscure the transcendent testimony of religion's founders and of the saints and sages who have followed after them—the shared truths that lie at the heart of all religions become clear. In these shared truths we find both an inspiring spiritual unity among all religions as well as ample room for the findings of science.

Together, the discoveries and theories of the broader minds of science and the testimony of the saints, sages, and near-death experiencers best reveal the physics of God. Material science is methodical and precise but can only confirm the truth of one detail at a time; it is unable to see the whole. The science of religion is methodical but less precise and yet able to see the whole. Together—the science of religion guiding the way, material science painstakingly confirming—science and religion give us the fullest picture of reality.

The Hidden Truth of Miracles: Matter Is the Intelligent Organization of Energy

Many religions and many scientists believe that the physical universe, especially matter, is a light-show illusion. Physicists have appreciated from the beginning of the 20th century that matter is not at all what it appears to be. Atoms are 99.9999 percent empty space. Further, the orbiting electrons that define the empty space of the atom and the tiny subatomic particles that make up the nucleus of the atom are, themselves, restless energy. Matter is not the fixed immutable substance that it appears to the senses. Matter is *intelligently organized invisible energy* moving in infinitesimally small patterns at the speed of light. This is said concisely and brilliantly in one of my favorite quotes, now familiar to you:

The visible world is the invisible organization of energy.

—Heinz Pagels, former executive director,
New York Academy of Sciences[3]

Many religions have long considered the physical world an illusion made of light. In Hinduism, Jainism, Sikhism, and Buddhism we find the concept of Maya: the world is a magic show, an illusion of cosmic light, in which things appear to be present but are not what they seem. "Let there be light," in the Judeo-Christian origin tradition strongly suggests that light is the foundation of matter. Before light, creation was "without form and void"; then God "breathed upon the face of the waters" (created vibrating waves of energy) that became light (electromagnetic energy).

Understanding matter's fundamentally ephemeral and mutable energy-based nature makes it easier to appreciate the lawful mechanism of miracles. We are confounded by miracles, whether unexplainable healings or such amazing manifestations as changing water to wine, because we do not see the workings of subtler laws of energy and thought that changed the hidden organization of the invisible energy. Nonetheless, abundant proof exists that we ourselves use these subtle laws of energy and thought routinely—from the instantaneous physiological changes of multiple personality sufferers, to placebo-induced self-healing, to the tiny but hugely statistically significant effect people can exert on the throw of dice. The dramatic miracles of the saints and sages are but the conscious and deliberate extension of the same hidden laws of energy and thought that we use—without knowing how we use them—every day.

Where the Heavens Lie: The Oceanic Energy-verse

According to M-theory, the most accepted version of string theory, most of the cosmos is a high-frequency energy realm—what I've been calling the energy-verse. The entire physical universe exists as a relatively tiny, three-dimensional space-time-and-matter bubble immersed in an effectively infinite ocean of energy. The ocean of energy is two-dimensional and nonlocal: without time, space, and matter.

What I call the "energy-verse" is referred to in M-theory as the "bulk," as in the "bulk of reality." The bulk is made up of layers or branes: separate, bounded energy-zones whose energies vibrate at different frequencies from those of other branes. It is not difficult mentally to correlate the differently vibrating energy branes that make up the bulk with the differently vibrating energy realms (heavens and hells) to which we go at death according to our own "vibration" or state of consciousness. All religious traditions describe multilayered realms—realms ranging from the highest heaven to the lowest hell—where souls go at death according to their behavior, their "vibration," achieved in this life.

> There are many different Heavens. . . . Everything is regulated by vibration, current and frequency. . . .
> —Christian Andréason, near-death experiencer[4]

The Heavens: Hologram for the Universe

M-theory's holographic principle states that all the *information* that organizes the energies that form the physical universe—including the natural laws that govern all matter-energy interactions and the entire history of matter-energy interactions going back to the Big Bang—resides in the interpenetrating, nonlocal energy-verse, not in the physical universe itself. This information exists in a hologram-like, dynamically evolving two-dimensional energy template that continuously projects the entire physical universe into being. Like the tiny dots that make up a newspaper image, ultra-tiny, subatomic-sized, three-dimensional, pure energy "dots" make up the universe.

The three-dimensional, true-to-all-five-senses, holographically projected cosmic movie we know as the physical universe arises from continuous interaction between the Intelligently guided nonlocal information hologram in the energy-verse—the heavens—and the unlimited energy of the energy-verse itself. Without the interpenetrating energies of the energy-verse interacting with the heavenly hologram, the physical universe could not exist. Without Intelligence guiding the heavenly hologram, the physical universe could not form coherently.

The blueprints of everything in the physical universe have been astrally conceived—all the forms and forces in nature, including the complex human body, have been first produced in that realm where God's causal ideations are made visible in forms of heavenly light and vibratory energy.

—Paramhansa Yogananda, yoga master[5]

Death Is a Shift in Awareness From the Physical Body to the Energy Body

Even at this moment, we live simultaneously in two realms—the physical universe and the energy-verse, which invisibly *interpenetrates* the physical universe at every point. The very high frequency at which the energies of the energy-verse vibrate—far higher even than that of gamma rays (the highest measurable frequency in three-dimensional space)—means that these high-frequency energies cannot be detected by our most finely calibrated measuring devices. Yet they are present everywhere. The entire physical universe is saturated, like a sponge in water, with the undetectable high-frequency energies poetically referred to by Wheeler as *quantum foam* and suggested by string theory's super-tiny vibrating rings and strings.

Until observed, potential matter exists as energy waves in this interpenetrating, nonlocal, high-frequency two-dimensional realm. When the matter-wave *is* observed and, as a result, behaves like a particle, the frequencies of the energy that makes up the particle it comprises vibrates at a lower, and therefore detectable, frequency. This change, however, is not permanent. Although matter-waves wink instantaneously into measureable matter form when observed, they can just as readily wink instantaneously back into energy waves.

Just as a two-dimensional, purely energy hologram contains the information that continuously projects the physical universe into being, so, too, we have our own personal two-dimensional purely energy hologram that contains the information that projects *our* physical body into being. Our personal two-dimensional energy body—variously called the astral body, light body, etheric body, spirit body, or subtle body—is the perfect, luminous counterpart of our physical body. Death, as the saints, sages, and near-death experiencers tell us, is only a shift from sensory awareness of our physical body to a more complete and more subtle awareness of our ever-present energy body.

Our energy body is constantly with us. It animates, controls, and continuously creates our physical body. Moreover, as the saints and sages tell us, our energy body contains what is most important, most characteristic, most essential; the things that give meaning to who and what we are: our thoughts, our feelings, our dreams, our knowledge, our memories, our enduring character traits. When we die, these essential aspects of who we are *continue* to exist where they have *always* existed—in our nonlocal energy body.

> In this way, our lives in this plane of existence are encompassed, surrounded, by the afterworld already. . . . The body dies but the spiritual quantum field continues. In this way, I am immortal.
>
> —Dr. Hans-Peter Dürr, former head of the
> Max Planck Institute for Physics, Munich[6]

The Secret of Life: Quantum Coherence

Many life processes—such as the body's recently discovered and mysterious ability to turn on and turn off genes, or the massive, and virtually instantaneous, coordination of quadrillions of life processes per second within the human body—cannot be fully explained by DNA preprogramming or by the relatively slow process of neuron signaling. Recent discoveries suggest that this intricate, intelligent coordination is instead the result of nonlocal information residing in our energy body controlling our physical body through quantum entanglement.

The new field of quantum biology—which surprised everyone with its discovery of chlorophyll's entangled, phased, and synchronized dance when transferring sunlight energy—has encountered *indefinitely sustained* states of entangled interaction bridging between the nonlocal energy-verse and living systems, an interaction known as *quantum coherence*. Quantum coherence is the key difference between living and non-living systems. It is no exaggeration to say that quantum coherence is the secret of life.

> [The body] would be rather like a beautiful, exotic flower, flickering in and out of many dimensions simultaneously.
> —Mae-Wan Ho, geneticist and quantum biologist[7]

> We are beginning to see the entire universe as a holographically interlinked network of energy and information, organically whole and self-referential at all scales of its existence. We, and all things in the universe, are non-locally connected with each other and with all other things in ways that are unfettered by the hitherto known limitations of space and time.
> —Ervin Laszlo, philosopher of science, author of
> *Cosmos: A Co-creator's Guide to the Whole-World*[8]

The Ultimate Common Ground: Consciousness Unites Science and Religion

In the early to mid-20th century, many physicists came to the conclusion that consciousness was the underlying foundation of reality. One of the most compelling reasons for this conclusion was the discovery of the intelligent-observer paradox. It can be argued that the paradox of the intelligent observer is to scientific materialism what the paradox of the constancy of the speed of light is to Newtonian physics.

Einstein's 1905 Special Theory of Relativity, a cornerstone proof of which is light's constant speed, revolutionized physics by revealing the *equivalence of matter and energy*—elegantly expressed in the equation $E = mc^2$. The paradigm-changing implications of Einstein's insights cannot be overstated. At the end of the 19th century, Newtonian physicists believed that space was infinite, that time was the same everywhere in the universe, and that matter was immutable. At the beginning of the 20th century, Einstein's equations proved that space is finite, that time is relative to the speed of the observer, and that matter is condensed energy.

The anomalous nature of the intelligent-observer effect has a similarly profound effect on scientific materialism. Its paradigm-changing implications, too, cannot be overstated. The intelligent-observer paradox turns scientific materialism on its head. The oft-demonstrated fact that the matter-wave will not behave as matter unless observed by an intelligent observer has led many eminent physicists to the conclusion that matter does not create consciousness—*consciousness creates matter.*

Although scientists and laymen alike find this principle difficult to embrace, some of the most important thinkers in physics (including Max Planck, David Bohm, Werner Heisenberg, Eugene Wigner, John Wheeler, John von Neumann, and Albert Einstein—who among them claim four Nobel Prizes in physics as well as every other elite award given to physicists and mathematicians) as well as a new generation of physicists (including Fritjof Capra, Amit Goswami, Gary Zukav, and Michio Kaku) have come to appreciate that scientific materialism is an incomplete system. In various ways, these physicists have seen the need for the presence of all-pervasive *intelligent consciousness* in order to provide a complete *scientific* explanation of reality.

The leap to embrace consciousness—science's farthest leap thus far—is the leap that nearly everyone finds the most difficult to make. Our resistance to the idea is more visceral than rational. Simply grasping the physical universe as a cosmic light projection is difficult enough; embracing the need for an ephemeral-seeming *consciousness* in order for the cosmic light show to exist at all demands a vastly greater imaginative reach.

Yet eminent scientists and mystics alike have arrived at this same conclusion. As quoted before:

> The stream of knowledge is heading toward a non-mechanical reality; the universe begins to look more like a great thought than like a great machine. Mind no longer appears to be an accidental intruder into the realm of matter, we ought rather hail it as the creator and governor of the realm of matter. Get over it, and accept the inarguable conclusion. The universe is immaterial-mental and spiritual.
>
> —Sir James Jeans, author of *The Mysterious Universe*[9]

God Is Pure, Intelligent Consciousness

> In whichever direction you may turn your gaze you will find One Eternal Invisible being manifested. Yet it is not all that easy to detect this presence, because He interpenetrates everything. . . . The analysis of the substance of all created things, if carried sufficiently far, will lead to the discovery that what remains is identical and equally present in all creatures: it is He, it is That, which is styled as Pure Consciousness.
>
> —Ananda Moyi Ma[10]

> To me it is clear that we exist in a plan which is governed by rules that were created, shaped by a universal intelligence and not by chance.
>
> —Michio Kaku, string theorist[11]

According to the saints and sages, creation begins with thought. God's intelligent laws are conceived in thought before the cosmos vibrates into being. Once conceived, these laws guide the unfolding behavior of creation, from the forming of the energy-verse and its heavens to the Big Bang, to the subsequent unfolding of the physical universe, to the eventual birth of life.

Scientific materialists strongly resist the concept of a guiding intelligence behind the formation of the cosmos. They prefer to think that the laws that govern the cosmos are purely accidental. Confronted with the astronomically high odds against our universe forming as it has by accident, scientific materialists have embraced the many-worlds interpretation: It provides a potential explanation for how our universe could have occurred randomly, without intelligent intention.

In the many-worlds interpretation, zillions of three-dimensional bubble universes randomly form out of the protean energy-verse, making it therefore inevitable that, out of the zillions of universes created, one would form as ours did. But the many-worlds interpretation endows *every possibility*—each and every one of the vast number of quantum possibilities that occur in each and every moment—with the causal power to create new, almost-identical copies of the *entire* universe from which that possibility emerged.

The many-worlds interpretation often makes me think of the old saying that some people lean so far backward to avoid falling forward that they fall over anyway. In scientific materialism's effort to avoid falling forward into embracing, even speculatively, the notion of nonmaterial intelligent consciousness, they have fallen over backward into a mathematical theory that reduces all of human life—from love to genius, from joy to transcendence—to fleetingly momentary accidents over which we have no influence whatsoever.

Take away the many-worlds interpretation, and its Darwinian explanation of our universe as the chance result of randomly mutating universes, and we are left with astronomical odds against our universe having developed accidentally. Without the many-worlds interpretation, it is hard *not* to conclude that the universe is tailor made.

Once we see, however, that the probability of life originating at random is so utterly miniscule as to make it absurd, it becomes sensible to think that the favorable properties of physics on which life depends are in every respect deliberate.... It is therefore almost inevitable that our own measure of intelligence must reflect . . . higher intelligences . . . even to the limit of God . . . such a theory is so obvious that one wonders why it is not widely accepted as being self-evident. The reasons are psychological rather than scientific.

—Fred Hoyle, mathematician and astronomer[12]

The Soul: Immortal and Godlike

Born of God, we are spirit, and cannot be anything else. All is mind—one mind. We are that mind asleep—yet awakening, and God is that mind eternally aware.

—Jan Price, near-death experiencer[13]

The saints, sages, and near-death experiencers not only testify that our universe is continuously created from the pure intelligent consciousness that is God, they tell us that we are immortal souls, made in His image of pure intelligent consciousness. We roam creation wearing various costumes of matter and energy: Our physical body is an expression of our interpenetrating, nonlocal, luminous energy body and our luminous energy body an expression of our interpenetrating thoughts.

That our deeply held thoughts have a particularly powerful effect on our physical bodies is remarkably well demonstrated by the placebo effect and by the numerous instantaneous physiological changes that take place when multiple-personality sufferers move from one personality to another: Scars and moles can appear or disappear; left-handedness can become right-handedness; visual acuity can increase or decrease; even eye color can change. Such phenomena strongly suggest that it is our deeper-than-conscious thoughts that shape and inform our personal, nonlocal, holographic energy template, which in turn shapes our physical body.

Matter responds, far more than most people realize, to the power of thought.

—Paramhansa Yogananda, yoga master[14]

Because no substance, however subtle, has been isolated and consistently measured by the instruments of science, the idea that thought exists outside the physical brain remains controversial; the idea is often labeled *paranormal* and pushed to the fringe of science. Nonetheless, compelling evidence indicates that our thoughts *are* communicated to others, regardless of distance, and that our thoughts *do* affect the outcome of physical processes. The evidence also suggests that thought, like the high-frequency energies of the energy-verse, is a nonlocal, interpenetrating phenomenon—undetectable and bound neither by space nor time but present everywhere.

The intelligent-observer effect further demonstrates the power we have over matter. Made in His image we share His abilities—our thoughts organize our nonlocal energy template, and then our energy template projects our body into physical form. Some few—the saints and sages—have learned, through disciplined meditation and profound inner absorption, not only how to wield this inherent ability to alter the holographically projected matter within their own bodies but also to alter, or even create, holographically projected matter outside their bodies.

God wants us to become as he is, and has invested us with godlike qualities. I understood that he wants us to draw on the powers of heaven, and that by believing we are capable of doing so, we can.

—Betty Eadie, near-death experiencer[15]

Miraculous abilities, however, do not express our highest potentials. Our highest potentials are discovered when we develop the ability to transcend the senses, to experience realities beyond sensory perception. Saints, sages, and near-death experiencers tell us that although the cosmic movie was created for our benefit, although we are endowed with the ability to alter the cosmic movie, in the end we weary of the show. Only by reuniting our consciousness completely with who and what we truly are can we ever be fully satisfied.

> Our hearts are restless until they find their rest in Thee.
>
> —St. Augustine[16]

Those who have actually achieved transcendence describe their experience of pure intelligent consciousness—movingly and personally—as an all-encompassing supernal light, an ecstasy of supreme joy, an immersion in pure and welcoming love, and an all-knowing compassion. They describe God as infinitely present and infinitesimally aware—an awe-inspiring intelligence that creates and sustains all of creation yet is at the same time intimately aware of their inmost thoughts.

Science and Religion—Together—Give Us a True Picture of Reality

Beneath the myriad trappings of religion we find the compellingly consistent testimony of the saints, sages, and near-death experiencers. In their transcendent awareness, they see the same vast, lawful, and subtle reality that open-minded quantum physicists, string theorists, quantum biologists, and neuroscientists painstakingly uncover through experimentation. The saints and sages add to the discoveries of modern scientists a breadth of vision that science has yet fully to achieve.

> The mystic and the physicist arrive at the same conclusion; one starting from the inner realm, the other from the outer world. The harmony between their views confirms the ancient Indian wisdom that Brahman, the ultimate reality without, is identical to Atman, the reality within.
>
> —Fritjof Capra, author of *The Tao of Physics*[17]

The testimony of the saints and sages does not counter the findings of science; it enlarges upon them. The workings of Consciousness are just as lawful as the workings of gravity. It is only because science has yet to understand those higher laws, known now only to men and women with direct transcendent experience, that scientific materialists dismiss the results of those laws as impossible.

> We ought to remember that religion uses language in quite a different way from science . . . we conclude that if religion does indeed deal with objective truths, it ought to adopt the same criteria of truth as science. The fact that religions through the ages have spoken in images, parables, and paradoxes means simply that there are no other ways of grasping the reality to which they refer. But that does not mean that it is not a genuine reality.
>
> —Neils Bohr, Nobel Prize winner and the
> Father of Quantum Physics[18]

> All creation is governed by law. The ones which manifest in the outer universe, discoverable by scientists, are called natural laws. But there are subtler laws ruling the realms of consciousness which can be known only through the inner science [of religion]. . . . The hidden spiritual planes also have their natural and lawful principles of operation.
>
> —Sri Yukteswar[19]

> There probably is a God. Many things are easier to explain if there is than if there isn't.
>
> —John Von Neumann, physicist and mathematician[20]

I hope that by now you can appreciate, if you hadn't before reading this book, that science and religion together give the most complete view of reality. Not only have we seen that the consistent testimony of the saints, sages, and near-death experiencers is congruent with science, we have seen that the timeless claims of all religions—miracles, life after death, heaven, God, and personal transcendent experience—find confirmation in scientific experiment or, barring full confirmation, find affirmation in numerous scientific theories.

I also hope that you can now separate the belief system of scientific materialism from the open-minded discovery process of science—and that you can separate the confusing trappings of religion from the science of religion.

Finally, I hope that you have found personal inspiration in the physics of God. Practices of the science of religion that lead to inner awakening—most notably meditation—will allow you to experience a joy beyond anything you've ever known.

We are far more than we know.

This was difficult for me to grasp in some places, but I think I got the gist of it. We all have God Consciousness to create our own world the way we want it. at the end of the day it is all about what we think, and what we think is true!!

NOTES

Introduction

1. Phillips, *Extra-Sensory Perception.*

Chapter 1

1. Tegmark, "Consciousness as a State."
2. Anthony, "Human Consciousness."
3. Francis, "Quantum and Consciousness."
4. Jahn and Dunne, *Quantum Mechanics.*
5. TED, "Graham Hancock."
6. Pew, "RELIGION AND SCIENCE."
7. Goswami, *Self-Aware Universe*, 60.
8. Herbert, *Quantum Reality*, 15.
9. Schlosshauer, Kofler, and Zeilinger, "Foundational Attitudes," 222–230.
10. Fielding et al., "Adjuvant chemotherapy," 390–399.
11. Coons, "Psychophysiologic Aspects," 47–53.
12. Shepard and Braun, "Visual Changes," 85.
13. Mumford, Rose, and Goshin, *Remote Viewing.*
14. Eddington, *Physical World*, 276–81.
15. Capra, *Tao of Physics*, 78.
16. Goswami, *Self-Aware Universe*, 10.
17. Einstein, *World As I See It*, 28–29.

Chapter 2

1. Easwaran, *Original Goodness*, 26.
2. Rūmī and Barks, *Essential Rumi*, 22.

3. Yogananda and Walters, *Essence of Self-Realization*, chapter 10, 9.
4. Spink, *Mother Teresa*, 39.
5. Newberg, D'Aquili, and Rause, *Why God*.
6. Peng et al., "Heart Rate Dynamics," 19–27.
7. Kothari, Bardia, and Gupta, "Yogic Claim," 282–284.
8. St. Teresa of Avila, *Interior Castle*.
9. Blofeld, *Zen Teaching*, 79.
10. Sivananda, "Peace of Mind."
11. Bush et al., "Anterior Cingulate Cortex," 215–222; Docety et al., "Functional Architecture," 71–100; Lutz et al., "Compassion Meditation."
12. Steiner and Bamford, *Higher Worlds*, 36.
13. Gallup and Proctor, *Adventures in Immortality*.
14. van Lommel et al., "Near-Death Experience," 2039–45.
15. Machado and Shewmon, *Brain Death*, 120.
16. Sharp, *After the Light*, 243.
17. Smith, "Moment of Truth."
18. Martin, *Searching for Home*, 27.
19. Rodonaia as quoted in Berman, *The Journey Home*, 34.
20. Umipeg as quoted in Ring and Cooper, *Mindsight*.
21. Andréason, "Near-Death Experience."
22. Dennis, *Pattern*, 40.
23. Alexander, *Proof of Heaven*, 130.
24. Brodsky as quoted in Ring and Valarino, *Lessons from the Light*, 299.
25. Benedict as quoted in Bailey, Worth, and Yates, *Near-Death Experience*, 49.
26. Yogananda, *Second Coming of Christ*.
27. Ivankovic-Mijatovic as quoted in Livio, "Description of Heaven."

Chapter 3

1. Pagels, *Cosmic Code*, 13.

Chapter 4

1. Wigner as quoted in BenDaniel, *On Wigner's Suggestion*, 1.
2. I found this quote by Heinrich Hertz in many reputable papers but could never track down the original source. Should any reader know of it, please contact the publisher listed on the copyright page of this book.
3. Dirac, "Picture of Nature."
4. Carroll, "Kos Science Panel."
5. Milonni, *Quantum Vacuum*.
6. Yukteswar as quoted in Yogananda, *Autobiography of a Yogi*, 263.
7. Spurgin, *Insights into the Afterlife*.
8. Yukteswar as quoted in Yogananda, *Autobiography of a Yogi*, 260.

9. Rodonaia as quoted in Berman, *The Journey Home*, 35.
10. Jung, *Memories, Dreams, Reflections*, 295.
11. Andréason, *www.near-death.com/andreason.html*.
12. Yogananda, *Autobiography of a Yogi*, 4.

Chapter 5

1. Swedenborg and Dole, *Heaven and Hell*, 57.
2. Yukteswar as quoted in Yogananda, *Autobiography of a Yogi*, 260.
3. Yogananda, "Astral World."
4. Eadie and Taylor, *Embraced by the Light*, 47–48.
5. Metaxas, "Case for God," 25.
6. Feynman, *Probability & Uncertainty*, 129.
7. Einstein, Born, and Born, *Born-Einstein Letters*.
8. Juan et al., "Bounding the speed," 614.
9. Matson, "Quantum Teleportation."
10. Bell, "Einstein Podolsky Rosen Paradox," 195–200.
11. Folger, "Quantum Shmantum," 37–43.
12. Bohm and Hiley, "Intuitive Understanding of Nonlocality," 93–109.
13. Bohm, *Implicate Order*, 11.
14. Englert et al., "Surrealistic Bohm Trajectories," 1175–1186.
15. Mahler et al., "Surreal Bohmian Trajectories."
16. Bohm, *Implicate Order*, xv.
17. "Top Cited Articles during 2010 in hep-th." Stanford University, Retrieved 25 July 2013, *www.slac.stanford.edu/spires/topcites/2010/eprints/to_hep-th _annual.shtml*
18. Jaggard, "What Is the Universe?"
19. Laszlo and Currivan, *Cosmos*, xiii.
20. Swedenborg, *Heaven and Hell,* 57.
21. Eadie, *Embraced by the light*, 47–48.
22. Yogananda, "The Astral World."
23. Eckhart and Fox, *Meditations with Meister Eckhart*, 24.
24. Swimme, *Hidden Heart of the Cosmos*, 100.
25. Suzuki, *Zen and Japanese culture*, 364.
26. Wiener, *Human Use of Human Beings*, 130.
27. Born, *Restless Universe*, Postscript.

Chapter 6

1. Yogananda, *Second Coming of Christ*, 10.
2. Linde et al., "Migraine Prophylaxis."
3. Cherkin et al., "Randomized trial," 858–66.
4. Bjordal et al., "Short-term efficacy," 51.

5. Trinh et al., "Lateral epicondyle pain," 1085–90.
6. Brennen as quoted in Dicarlo, "New World View."
7. Besant, *Karma*, Sec 13.
8. Chinmoy, *Jewels of Happiness*, Chapter 1.
9. Chow, "DNA May Not Be Your Destiny."
10. Baltimore, "Our Genome Unveiled," 814–816.
11. Lipton, *Biology of Belief*, 33–34.
12. Lalande, "Parental Imprinting," 173–195.
13. Ornish et al., "Changes in Prostate Gene," 8369–8374.
14. Rönn et al., "Six Months Exercise Intervention."
15. Engel et al., "Evidence for Wavelike Energy," 782–786.
16. Ho et al., "Organisms as Polyphasic Liquid Crystals, 81–91.
17. Lipton, *Biology of Belief*, 46–47.
18. Cabral, "Oscillatory dynamics," 402–415.
19. Fraccia et al., "Abiotic ligation of DNA.".
20. Ho, *Bioenergetics and Biocommunication*.
21. Yukteswar as quoted in Yogananda, *Autobiography of a Yogi*, 76.
22. Carrel, *Man, the Unkown*.
23. Hebb, *Textbook of Psychology*.
24. Coons, "Psychophysiologic Aspects."
25. Pagels, *Cosmic Code*, 13.
26. Atwater, *Beyond the Light*, 182.
27. Williams, "Near-Death Experience."
28. Dennis, *Pattern*, 29.

Chapter 7

1. Luparello et al., "Influences of Suggestion," 819–829.
2. Fielding, "An interim report," 390–399.
3. Moseley et al., "Controlled trial of arthroscopic surgery," 81–88.
4. Radin, *Entangled minds*, 129.
5. Ibid., 149.
6. Wiseman as quoted in Oenman, "Could there be proof?"
7. Schlosshauer et al., "Foundational Attitudes."
8. Goswami, *Self-Aware Universe*, 60.
9. Wigner et al., *Philosophical Reflections and Syntheses*, 14.
10. Schrödinger, *Mind and Matter*.
11. Davies, *Other Worlds*, 126.
12. Bohm, *Implicate Order*, 3
13. Einstein, Dyson, and Calaprice, *New Quotable Einstein*, 206.
14. Heisenberg, *Physics and philosophy*, 154.
15. Dossey, *Science of Premonitions*, 191.
16. *Observer*, 25 January 1931.

17. Jeans, *Mysterious universe*, 137.
18. Kaku as quoted in Connolly, "World renown scientist."
19. Russell and Russell, *Universal Law*, Prelude.
20. Atwater, *Beyond the light*, 185.
21. Kriyananda and Yogananda, *Bhagavad Gita*, Stanza 30.
22. Jeans, *Mysterious Universe*, 137.

Chapter 8

1. Linde as quoted in Folger, "Quantum Shmantum."
2. Wheeler as quoted in Zurek, "Physics of Information," 5.
3. Goswami, *Self-Aware Universe*, 60.
4. Byrom, *Dhammapada*.
5. Yogananda, *Divine Romance*, 31.
6. Yogananda, *Autobiography of a Yogi*, 172.
7. Sasaki and Farkas, *Zen Eye*, 41.
8. Price, *Other Side of Death*, 63.
9. Tennyson and Roberts, *Major Works*, 520.
10. Bucke, *Cosmic Consciousness*, 9–10.
11. Lionel, *Seduction of the Occult Path*.
12. Russell and Russell, *Universal Law*, Prelude.
13. Atwater, *Beyond the Light*, 142.
14. Echart et al., *Meister Eckhart*, 153.
15. Sivananda, "Cosmic Consciousness."
16. St. Teresa of Avila, 412-424.
17. Govinda, *Foundations of Tibetan Mysticism*, 305.
18. Richard, *De Quatuor*, cxcvi.
19. Thomas, *Moral teaching of St. Thomas*, xlvii.
20. Yogananda, *Autobiography of a Yogi*, 93.
21. Linde as quoted in Folger, "Quantum Shmantum."
22. Wheeler as quoted in Zurek, "Complexity," 5.
23. Goswami, *Self-Aware Universe*, 60.
24. Byrom, *Dhammapada*.

Chapter 9

1. Hildebrand, "Das Universum," 10.
2. Yogananda, *Autobiography of a Yogi*, 171.
3. Pagels, *The cosmic code*, 13.
4. Andréason, www.near-death.com/andreason.html.
5. Yogananda, "The Astral World."
6. Durr, Television Interview.
7. Ho, "Quantum Coherence."

8. Laszlo, *Cosmos*, xiii.
9. Jeans, *Mysterious Universe*, 137.
10. Ma as quoted in Conway, *Women of Power*, 152.
11. Kaku as quoted in Connolly, "World renown scientist."
12. Hoyle and Wickramasinghe, *Evolution from Space*, 141, 144, 130.
13. Price, *Other side of death*, 63.
14. Yogananda, *Karma and Reincarnation*.
15. Eadie, *Embraced by the Light*, 61.
16. Augustine and Pusey, "Confessions of St. Augustine," 1.
17. Capra, *Tao of Physics*, 305.
18. Bohr as quoted in Heisenberg, *On Modern Physics*.
19. Yukteswar as quoted in Yogananda, *Autobiography of a Yogi*, 74.
20. Von Neumann as quoted in Macrae, *Scientific Genius*, 379.

BIBLIOGRAPHY

Alexander, Eben. *Proof of Heaven: A Neurosurgeon's Journey Into the Afterlife*. New York: Simon & Schuster, 2012.

Andréason, Christian. *Christian Andréason's Near-Death Experience*. Accessed October 7, 2015. *www.near-death.com/experiences/notable /christian-andreason.html*.

Anthony, Sebastian. "Human consciousness Is Simply a State of Matter, Like Solid or Liquid—but Quantum," *ExtremeTech*, April 24, 2014, *www .extremetech.com/extreme/181284-human-consciousness-is-simply-a -state-of-matter-like-a-solid-or-liquid-but-quantum*.

Atwater, P.M.H. *Beyond the Light: What Isn't Being Said About Near-Death Experience*. New York: Carol Publishing Group, 1994.

Augustine, and E.B. Pusey. *The Confessions of St. Augustine*. Waiheke Island: Floating Press, 2008.

Bailey, Lee Worth, and Jenny L. Yates. *The Near-Death Experience: A Reader*. New York: Routledge, 1996.

Baltimore, David. "Our genome unveiled," *Nature* 409, no. 6822 (2001): 814–816.

Bell, John. "On the Einstein Podolsky Rosen Paradox," *Physics* 1, no. 3 (1964): 195–200.

BenDaniel, David J., *On Wigner's Suggestion of the Unreasonable Effectiveness of Mathematics in the Natural Sciences.* Ithaca, N.Y.: Cornell University, Johnson Graduate School of Management, 1993.

Berman, Phillip L. *The Journey Home: What Near-Death Experiences and Mysticism Teach Us About the Gift of Life.* New York: Pocket Books, 1996.

Besant, Annie. *Karma.* Los Angeles: Theosophical Publishing House, 1918.

Bjordal, J.M., M.I. Johnson, R.A. Lopes-Martins, B. Bogen, R. Chow, A.E. Ljunggren. "Short-term efficacy of physical interventions in osteoarthritic knee pain. A systematic review and meta-analysis of randomised placebo-controlled trials," *BMC Musculoskelet Disord* 22, no. 8 (2007): 51.

Blofeld, John. *The Zen Teaching of Huang Po on the Transmission of Mind.* 1958.

Bohm, D.J., and B.J. Hiley. "On the intuitive understanding of nonlocality as implied by quantum theory," *Foundations of Physics: An International Journal Devoted to the Conceptual Bases and Fundamental Theories of Modern Physics, Biophysics and Cosmology* 5, no. 1 (1975): 93–109.

Bohm, David. *Wholeness and the Implicate Order.* London: Routledge & Kegan Paul, 1980.

Born, Max. *The Restless Universe.* New York: Dover Publications, 1951.

Brennan, Barbara. *Conversations Toward a new World View: Exploring the Human Energy System Interview with Barbara Brennan PhD.* n.d. *www.healthy.net/scr/Interview.aspx?Id=165.*

Bucke, Richard Maurice. *Cosmic Consciousness: A Study in the Evolution of the Human Mind.* New York: Dutton, 1969.

Bush, George, Phan Luu, and Michael I. Posner. "Cognitive and emotional influences in anterior cingulate cortex," *Trends in Cognitive Sciences* 4, no 6 (2000): 215–222.

Byrom, Thomas. *Dhammapada: The Sayings of the Buddha.* Berkeley, Calif.: Shambala Pub, 1993.

Cabral, et al. "Oscillatory dynamics and place field maps reflect sequence and place memory processing in hippocampal ensembles under NMDA receptor control," *Neuron* 81, no. 2 (2014): 402–415.

Capra, Fritjof. *The Tao of Physics: An Exploration of the Parallels Between Modern Physics and Eastern Mysticism.* Berkeley, Calif.: Shambhala, 1975.

————. *The Turning Point: Science, Society, and the Rising Culture.* New York: Simon and Schuster, 1982.

Carrel, Alexis. *Man, the Unkown.* London: Hamish Hamilton, 1942.

Carroll, Sean. "Yearly Kos Science Panel." California Institute of Technology. Part 1. 2006.

Cherkin, D.C, K.J. Sherman, A.L. Avins, J.H. Erro, L. Ichikawa, W.E. Barlow, K. Delaney, R. Hawkes, L. Hamilton, A. Pressman, P.S. Khalsa, and R.A. Deyo. "A randomized trial comparing acupuncture, simulated acupuncture, and usual care for chronic low back pain," *Arch Intern Med* 11, no. 169 (2009): 858–66.

Chiesa, A., et al. "A systematic review of neurobiological and clinical features of mindfulness meditations." *Psychological Medicine*, 40, no. 40 (n.d.): 1239–1252.

Chinmoy, Sri. *The Jewels of Happiness.* London: Watkins Publishing, 2010.

Chow, Denise. "Why Your DNA May Not Be Your Destiny." *LiveScience.* June 4, 2015. Accessed November 10, 2015. *www.livescience.com/37135 -dna-epigenetics-disease-research.html.*

Connolly, Marshall. "World renown scientist says he has found proof of God! We may be living the the 'Matrix,'" *Catholic Online.* June 8, 2016. Accessed July 10, 2016. http://www.catholic.org/news/technology /story.php?id=69335.

Conway, Timothy. *Women of Power and Grace: Nine Astonishing, Inspiring Luminaries of Our Time.* Santa Barbara, Calif.: Wake Up Press, 1994.

Coons, Philip M. "Psychophysiologic Aspects of Multiple Personality Disorder, A Review. Dissociation," *Ridgeview Institute and the International Society for the Study of Multiple Personality & Dissociation* 1, no. 1 (n.d.): 047–053.

Davies, P.C.W. *Other Worlds: A Portrait of Nature in Rebellion, Space, Superspace, and the Quantum Universe.* New York: Simon and Schuster, 1980.

Dennis, Lynnclaire. *The Pattern.* Lower Lake, Calif.: Integral Publishing, 1997.

Dicarlo, Russell. "Conversations Toward a New World View: Exploring the Human Energy System." *healthy.net* n.d. *www.healthy.net/scr/Interview.aspx?Id=165.*

Dirac, P.A.M. "The Evolution of the Physicist's Picture of Nature," *Scientific American* 208, no. 5 (1963): 45–53.

Docety J, et al. "The Functional Architecture of Human Empathy," *Behavioral and Cognitive Neuroscience Reviews* 3, no. 2 (2004): 71–100.

Dossey, Larry. *The Science of Premonitions: How Knowing the Future Can Help Us Avoid Danger, Maximize Opportunities, and Create a Better Life.* New York: Plume, 2010.

Dunne, Robert, G. Jahn, PhD, and Brenda J. *Margins of Reality: The Role of Consciousness.* Orlando, Florida: Harcourt Brace & Company, 1987.

Durr, Hans-Peter. "Television Interview," *PM Magazine* May, 2007.

Eadie, Betty J., and Curtis Taylor. *Embraced by the Light.* Placerville, Calif.: Gold Leaf Press, 1992.

Easwaran, Eknath. *Original Goodness.* Petaluma, Calif.: Nilgiri Press, 1989.

Eckhart, and Matthew Fox. *Meditations with Meister Eckhart.* Sante Fe, N.M.: Bear & Co., 1983.

Eckhart, Meister, C. de B. Evans, Franz Pfeiffer, and Meister Eckhart. *Meister Eckhart.* London: J.M. Watkins, 1952.

Eddington, Arthur Stanley. *The Nature of the Physical World.* New York: Macmillan Co., 1928.

Einstein, Albert. *The World As I See It.* New York: Philosophical Library, 1949.

Einstein, Albert, Freeman Dyson, and Alice Calaprice. *The New Quotable Einstein.* Princeton: Princeton University Press, 2005.

Einstein, Albert, Max Born, and Hedwig Born. *The Born-Einstein Letters; Correspondence Between Albert Einstein and Max and Hedwig Born from 1916 to 1955*. New York: Walker, 1971.

Engel, Gegory, et al. "Evidence for wavelike energy transfer through quantum coherence in photosynthetic systems," *Nature* 446 (2007): 782–786.

Englert, Berthold-Georg, Marian O. Scully, Georg Sussmann, and Herbert Walther. "Surrealistic Bohm Trajectories," *Zeitschrift Fur Naturforschung A* 47, no. 12 (1992).

Feynman, Richard P. *Probability & Uncertainty the Quantum Mechanical View of Nature*. Newton, Mass: Education Development Center, 1990.

Fielding, J.W.L., S.L. Fagg, B.G. Jones, D. Ellis, M.S. Hockey, A. Minawa, V.S. Brookes, et al.. "An interim report of a prospective, randomized, controlled study of adjuvant chemotherapy in operable gastric cancer: British stomach cancer group," *World Journal of Surgery* 7, no. 3 (1983): 390–399.

Folger, T. "Quantum Shmantum," *Discover* 22 (2001): 37–43.

———. "Does the Universe Exist if We're Not Looking?" *Discover*. June 1, 2002. Accessed May 16, 2016. *http://discovermagazine.com/2002/jun/featuniverse*.

Fraccia, Tommaso P., et al. "Abiotic ligation of DNA oligomers templated by their liquid crystal ordering." *Nature Communications* 6, Article 6424 (2015).

Francis, Matthew R. "Quantum and Consciousness Often Mean Nonsense," *Slate*, May 29, 2014, *www.slate.com/articles/health_and_science/science/2014/05/quantum_consciousness_physics_and_neuroscience_do_not_explain_one_another.html*.

Gallup, George, and William Proctor. *Adventures in Immortality*. New York: McGraw-Hill, 1982.

Goswami, Amit. *The Self-Aware Universe*. New York: Putnam's Sons, 1993.

Govinda, Anagarika. *Foundations of Tibetan Mysticism: According to the Esoteric Teachings of the Great Mantra, Om Mani Padme Hūm*. York Beach, Maine: Samuel Weiser, Inc., 1969.

Hawking, Stephen, and Leonard Mlodinow. *The Grand Design*. New York: Bantam Books, 2010.

Hebb, D.O. *A Textbook of Psychology*. Philadelphia: Saunders, 1966.

Heisenberg, Werner. *On Modern Physics*. New York: C.N. Potter., 1961.

———. *Physics and Philosophy: The Revolution in Modern Science*. New York: Harper, 1958.

Herbert, Nick. *Quantum Reality: Beyond the New Physics*. Garden City, N.Y.: Anchor Press/Doubleday, 1985.

Hildebrand, Ulrich. "Das Universumû—Hinweis auf Gott?" *Ethos. Die Zeitschrift für die ganze Familie*, 10 (1988).

Ho, Mae-Wan. *Bioenergetics and Biocommunication*. 1996. Accessed November 2015. *www.ratical.org/co-globalize/MaeWanHo/biocom95.html*.

Ho, Mae-Wan. "Quantum Coherence and Conscious Experience." 1997. *Institute of Science in Society https://ratical.org/co-globalize/MaeWanHo/brainde.html*.

Ho, Mae-Wan, et al. "Organisms as polyphasic liquid crystals," *Bioelectrochemistry and Bioenergetics* 41, no. 1 (1996): 81–91.

Hoyle, Fred, and N. Chandra Wickramasinghe. *Evolution from Space*. London: J.M. Dent & Sons, 1981.

Huangbo, and Xiu Pei. *The Zen Teaching of Huang Po on the Transmission of Mind; Being the Teaching of the Zen Master Huang Po as Recorded by the Scholar P'ei Hsiu of the T'ang Dynasty*. New York: Grove Press, 1959.

Jaggard, Victoria. "What Is the Universe? Real Physics Has Some Mind-Bending Answers." *Smithsonian.com* 2014. *www.smithsonianmag.com/science/what-universe-real-physics-has-some-mind-bending-answers-180952699/?no-ist*.

Jahn, Robert G., and Brenda J. Dunne. *On the quantum mechanics of consciousness, with application to anomalous phenomena*. Princeton, N.J.: Princeton Engineering Anomalies Research Laboratory, School of Engineering/Applied Science, Princeton University, 1984.

Jalāl al-Dīn Rūmī, and Coleman Barks. *The Essential Rumi.* San Francisco: Harper, 1995.

Jalāl al-Dīn Rūmī, and Shahram Shiva. *Hush, Don't Say Anything to God: Passionate Poems of Rumi.* Fremont, Calif.: Jain Publishing, 2000.

Jeans, James. *The Mysterious Universe.* New York: The Macmillan Company, 1932.

Juan Yin, et al. "Bounding the speed of 'spooky action at a distance.'" Phys. Rev. Lett. 110, 260407 1303: 614. arXiv:1303.0614. Bibcode:2013arXiv1303.0614Y. 2013.

Jung, C.G. *Memories, Dreams, Reflections.* New York: Pantheon Books, 1963.

Kothari L.K., A. Bardia, and O.P. Gupta. "The yogic claim of voluntary control over the heart beat: an unusual demonstration," *American Heart Journal* 86, no. 2 (1973): 282–4.

Kriyananda, and Yogananda. *The Essence of the Bhagavad Gita.* Nevada City, Calif.: Crystal Clarity Publishers, 2006.

Lalande, M. "Parental imprinting and human disease," *Annual Review of Genetics* 30 (1996): 173–195.

Laszlo, Ervin and Jude Currivan. *Cosmos: A Co-creator's Guide to the Whole-World.* ReadHowYouWant, 2013.

Linde, K., G. Allais, B. Brinkhaus, E. Manheimer, A. Vickers, A.R. White. "Acupuncture for migraine prophylaxis," *Cochrane Database Syst Rev* 21, no. 1 (2009): CD001218.

Lionel, Frédéric. *The Seduction of the Occult Path: Encounters on the Road to Inner Transformation.* Wellingborough: Turnstone, 1983.

Lipton, Ph.D., Bruce H. *The Biology of Belief.* Carlsbad, Calif.: Hay House, Kindle Edition, 2008.

Livio, Fr. *Description of heaven.* n.d. *www.medjugorje.com/medjugorje /heaven-purgatory-hell/613-description-of-heaven.html.*

Luparello, T., H.A. Lyons, E.R. Bleecker, et al. "Influences of Suggestion on Airway Reactivity in Asthmatic Subjects," *Psychosomatic Medicine* 30, no. 6 (1968): 819–829.

Lutz, A., et al. "Regulation of the Neural Circuitry of Emotion by Compassion Meditation: Effects of Meditative Expertise," n.d. *PLoS ONE 3(3) e1897.*

Mahler, D.H., L. Rozema, K. Fisher, L. Vermeyden, K.J. Resch, H.M. Wiseman, and A. Steinberg. "Experimental nonlocal and surreal Bohmian trajectories," *Science Advances* 2, no. 2 (2016): e1501466.

Martin, Laurelynn G. *Searching for Home: A Personal Journey of Transformation and Healing After a Near-Death Experience.* Saint Joseph, Mich.: Cosmic Concepts, 1996.

Matson, John. "Quantum teleportation achieved over record distances," *Nature* (2012).

Machado, C. and Shewmon. *Brain Death and Disorders of Consciousness.* New York: Kluwer Academic/Plenum Publishers, 2004.

Metaxas, Eric. "Science Increasingly Makes the Case for God." *Wall Street Journal Opinion*, December 25, 2014.

Milonni, Peter W. *The Quantum Vacuum: An Introduction to Quantum Electrodynamics.* Boston: Academic Press, 1994.

Moseley J.B., K. O'Malley, N.J. Petersen, T.J. Menke, B.A. Brody, D.H. Kuykendall, J.C. Hollingsworth, C.M. Ashton, and N.P. Wray. "A controlled trial of arthroscopic surgery for osteoarthritis of the knee," *The New England Journal of Medicine* 347, no. 2 (2002): 81–88.

Mumford, Michael D., Andrew H. Rose, David A. Goshin, and American Institutes for Research. *An Evaluation of Remote Viewing: Research and Applications.* Palo Alto, Calif.: American Institutes for Research, 1995.

Newberg, Andrew B., Eugene G. D'Aquili, and Vince Rause. *Why God Won't Go Away: Brain Science and the Biology of Belief.* New York: Ballantine Books, 2001.

Oenman, Danny. *Could there be proof to the theory that we're ALL psychic?* January 28, 2008. Accessed January 21, 2016. *www.daily mail.co.uk/news/article-510762/Could-proof-theory-ALL-psychic.html #ixzz3jSzcXws7.*

Ornish, D., M.J. Magbanua, G. Weidner, et al. "Changes in Prostate Gene Expression in Men Undergoing an Intensive Nutrition and Lifestyle Intervention," *Proceedings of the National Academy of Sciences* 105, no. 24 (2008): 8369–8374.

Pagels, Heinz R. *The Cosmic Code: Quantum Physics as the Language of Nature.* New York: Simon and Schuster, 1982.

Peng C.K, I.C. Henry, J.E. Mietus, J.M. Hausdorff, G. Khalsa, H. Benson, and A.L. Goldberger. "Heart rate dynamics during three forms of meditation," *International Journal of Cardiology* 95, no. 1 (2004): 19–27.

Pew. "RELIGION AND SCIENCE IN THE UNITED STATES: Scientists and Belief." *OewResearchCenter.* November 5, 2009. Accessed October 7, 2015. www.pewforum.org/2009/11/05/scientists-and-belief/.

Phillips, Stephen M. *Extra-sensory Perception of Quarks.* Madras, India: Theosophical Publishing House, 1980.

Price, Jan. *The Other Side of Death.* New York: Fawcett Columbine, 1996.

Radin, Dean I. *Entangled Minds: Extrasensory Experiences in a Quantum Reality.* New York: Paraview Pocket Books, 2006.

Richard of St Victor. *De Quatuor Gradibus Violentae Charitatis.* migne. n.d.

Ring, Kenneth, and Evelyn Elsaesser Valarino. *Lessons From the Light: What We Can Learn from the Near-Death Experience.* New York: Insight Books, 1998.

Ring, Kenneth, and Sharon Cooper. *Mindsight: Near-Death and Out-of-Body Experiences in the Blind.* Palo Alto, Calif.: William James Center for Consciousness Studies, 1999.

Rönn, T., P. Volkov, C. Davegårdh, et al. "A Six Months Exercise Intervention Influences the Genome-Wide DNA Methylation Pattern in Human Adipose Tissue," *PLOS Genetics* 9, no. 6 (2013): e1003572.

Russell, Walter, Lao Russell. *Universal Law, Natural Science and Philosophy.* Waynesboro, Va.: The Walter Russell Foundation, 1950.

Sasaki, Shigetsu, and Mary Farkas. *The Zen Eye: A Collection of Zen Talks by Sokei-an.* Tokyo: Weatherhill, 1993.

Schlosshauer, Maximilian, Johannes Kofler, and Anton Zeilinger. "A snapshot of foundational attitudes toward quantum mechanics," *Studies in History and Philosophy of Modern Physics* 44, no. 3 (2013): 222–230.

Schrödinger, Erwin. *Mind and Matter.* Cambridge, U.K.: University Press, 1958.

Sharp, Kimberly Clark. *After the Light: What I Discovered on the Other Side of Life That Can Change Your World.* New York: William Morrow and Co, 1995.

Shepard, K.R., and B.G. Braun. "Visual changes in multiple personality." *PROCEEDINGS OF THE SECOND INTERNATIONAL CONFERENCE ON MULTIPLE PERSONALITY/DISSOCIATIVE STATES.* Chicago, Rush-Presbyterian-St Luke's Medical Center. 85. 1985.

Sivananda, Swami. "Cosmic Consciousness." *The Divine Life Society.* n.d. *www.sivanandaonline.org/public_html/?cmd=displaysection&section_id=1727.*

———. *How to Find Peace of Mind.* n.d. Accessed October 7, 2015. *www.sivanandaonline.org/public_html/?cmd=displaysection&section_id=848.*

Smith, Jayne. "Moment of Truth: A Window On Life After Death." *Video transcript.* Starpath Productions, 1987.

Spink, Kathryn. *Mother Teresa: A Complete Authorized Biography.* San Francisco: HarperSanFrancisco, 1997.

Spurgin, Nora M. *Insights into the Afterlife: 30 Questions on What to Expect.* New York: Womans Federation of World Peace, 1994.

Steiner, Rudolf, and Christopher Bamford. *How to Know Higher Worlds: A Modern Path of Initiation.* Hudson, N.Y.: Anthroposophic Press, 1994.

St. Teresa of Avila. *Interior Castle.* Grand Rapids, Mich.: Christian Classics Ethereal Library, 1990.

Suzuki, Daisetz Teitaro. *Zen and Japanese Culture.* New York: Pantheon Books, 1959.

Swedenborg, Emanuel, and George F. Dole. *Heaven and Hell.* New York: Swedenborg Foundation, 1984.

Swimme, Brian. *The Hidden Heart of the Cosmos*. New York: Orbis Books, 1996.

TED, Staff. "The debate about Graham Hancock's talk." *TEDBlog*. March 19, 2013. Accessed October 7, 2015. http://blog.ted.com/the -debate-about-graham-hancocks-talk/.

Tegmark, Max. "Consciousness as a State of Matter," *Cornell University Library* arXiv.org/quant-ph/arXiv. 2014. doi: 1401.1219.

Tennyson, Alfred Tennyson, and Adam Roberts. *The Major Works*. Oxford: Oxford University Press, 2009.

Teresa. *Interior Castle*. Grand Rapids, Mich.: Christian Classics Ethereal Library, 1990.

The Observer. 1931. January 25.

Thomas, and Joseph Rickaby. *Aquinas ethicus, or, The moral teaching of St. Thomas. A Translation of the Principle Portions of the Second Part of the "Summa theological," With Notes*. London: Burns and Oates, 1896.

Trinh, K.V., S.D. Phillips, Ho E., K. Damsma. "Acupuncture for the alle-viation of lateral epicondyle pain: a systematic review," *Rheumatology* 43, no. 9 (2004): 1085–90.

Tsu, Lao. *Tao Te Ching*. Translated by Gia-Fu Feng and Jane English. New York: Vintage Books, 1972.

van Lommel, P., R. van Wees, V. Meyers, and I. Elfferich. "Near-death experience in survivors of cardiac arrest: a prospective study in the Netherlands," *Lancet* 358, no. 9298 (2001): 2039–45.

Wiener, Norbert. *The Human Use of Human Beings*. New York: Avon Books, 1954.

Wigner, Eugene Paul, Jagdish Mehra, and A.S. Wightman. *Philosophical Reflections and Syntheses*. Berlin: Springer, 1995.

Williams, Kevin. *Heaven and the near-Death Experience*. n.d. Accessed November 11, 2015. *www.near-death.com/science/research/heaven .html*.

Wolf, Fred Alan. *Taking the Quantum Leap: The New Physics for Nonscientists*. San Francisco: Harper & Row, 1981.

Yin, Juan, et al. "Bounding the speed of spooky action at a distance," *Physical Review Letters* 260407, no. 1303 (2013): 614.

Yogananda. *Self-Realization Magazine* Spring/Summer. 2010.

———. *Karma and Reincarnation*. Nevada City, Calif.: Crystal Clarity Publishers, 2006.

———. "The Astral World." *Self-Realization Magazine*, Spring/Summer. 2010.

———. *The Divine Romance*. Los Angeles: Self-Realization Fellowship, 1986.

———. *The Second Coming of Christ: The Resurrection of the Christ Within You: A Revelatory Commentary on the Original Teachings of Jesus*. Los Angeles: Self-Realization Fellowship, 2004.

Yogananda, and J. Donald Walters. *The Essence of Self-Realization: The Wisdom of Paramhansa Yogananda*. Nevada City, Calif.: Crystal Clarity, 1990.

Yogananda, Paramhansa. *Autobiography of a Yogi*. Nevada City, Calif.: Crystal Clarity, 1946.

Zurek, Wojciech Hubert. "Complexity, entropy, and the physics of information: the proceedings of the 1988 Workshop on Complexity, Entropy, and the Physics of Information," *Workshop on Complexity, Entropy, and the Physics of Information*. Santa Fe, N.M.: Addison-Wesley Publishing Company, 1990.

INDEX

Index

Index

ABOUT THE AUTHOR

 Joseph Selbie makes the complex and obscure simple and clear. A dedicated meditator for more than 40 years, he has taught yoga and meditation throughout the United States and Europe. He has also been an avid follower of the unfolding new paradigm of science with groaning book shelves to show for it, and he is known for creating bridges of understanding between the modern evidence-based discoveries of science and the ancient experience-based discoveries of the mystics.

Selbie maintains several blogs, including Intersections, which explores how spirituality connects with culture and science. He has also authored *The Yugas*, a factual look at India's tradition of cyclical history, and a sci-fi fantasy series, *The Protectors Diaries*, inspired by the abilities of mystics.

Selbie is a founding member of Ananda, a meditation-based community and spiritual movement inspired by Paramhansa Yogananda. He lives with his wife at Ananda Village near Nevada City, California.

You can visit his website at *www.physicsandgod.com.*